Functional Grammar
and
Spoken and Written Communication in English

A STUDENT-FRIENDLY EDITION

Bikram K Das

Orient BlackSwan

FUNCTIONAL GRAMMAR AND SPOKEN AND WRITTEN
COMMUNICATION IN ENGLISH

ORIENT BLACKSWAN PRIVATE LIMITED

Registered Office
3-6-752 Himayatnagar, Hyderabad 500 029, Telangana, India
e-mail: centraloffice@orientblackswan.com

Other Offices
Bengaluru, Bhopal, Chennai, Guwahati, Hyderabad, Jaipur, Kolkata
Lucknow, Mumbai, New Delhi, Noida, Patna, Visakhapatnam

First published 2006
Reprinted 2007, 2008, 2009, 2011, 2013, 2014, 2015, 2017, 2018, 2019, 2020

Cover and book design

ISBN: 978 81 250 3058 4

Typeset in Times 11/13 *by*
OSDATA
Hyderabad 500 029

Printed in India at
The Print Park, Chennai 600 117

Published by
Orient Blackswan Private Limited
3-6-752, Himayatnagar, Hyderabad 500 029, Telangana, India
e-mail: info@orientblackswan.com

Contents

Preface

Functional Grammar and Spoken and Written Communication in English is designed for use as a textbook for English Paper II ('Novel, Functional Grammar and Communicative Skills') in the first year of the undergraduate degree programmes offered by the University of Kerala. Its content is based on the prescribed syllabus, and the topics for study as well as the exercises in the book have been patterned after the model question paper which is being followed. The larger objective of the book, however, is to equip undergraduate students with a comprehensive understanding of the important aspects of English that will allow them to communicate effectively in the language.

The book has five chapters, covering grammar, pronunciation, reading comprehension and vocabulary, written communication and spoken communication. Besides offering learners guidance on major topics and important points relating to its area, every chapter in the book offers support in the form of examples of sounds and grammatical structures as well as samples of the use of English to communicate in different situations and in performing important language functions. In addition, the book includes a large number of exercises that the student and the teacher will find useful as a means of enabling valuable language practice.

The texts in the book, including the illustrative sentences in the grammar section, the passages used for providing practice in reading comprehension, the sample letters and the paragraphs in the writing section as well as the dialogues in the speaking section, are all based on themes and contexts that are topical, and that students will be familiar with. A lot of thinking has gone into this aspect of the writing of the book so as to ensure that the students, in the course of learning English and improving their communicative skills in the language, enjoy using the book.

There are three appendices in the book. The first of these is a list of incorrect sentences, containing errors that Indian users of English commonly make, together with their corrections. This can be used for quick reference as well as for practice in correct usage. The second appendix is an introductory note on soft skills, which when combined with the course on essential language skills offered in the book, will be of relevance to undergraduate students, on the threshold of their careers. The third appendix is a key to the grammar and pronunciation exercises in the book. This has been included for easy access to a reference point that students can depend on in order to check their work and to correct themselves.

To conclude, although *Functional Grammar and Spoken and Written Communication in English* is primarily intended to meet specific syllabus requirements, the book can also help students improve their general skills in English and use the language with ease and confidence in different situations and to perform a range of communicative functions. It is hoped that the book will serve equally well both the purposes for which it has been written.

Bikram K. Das
June 2006

1 Grammar

The Importance of Grammar

In order to speak or write English effectively, it is necessary to use the language correctly. Each language has its own rules of correctness, which are known as rules of grammar. Indian learners who are not sure of the grammar of English often make mistakes while using English. In this part of the book, therefore, we will quickly go over some selected areas of English grammar which are known to cause difficulties to learners, in order to help you avoid some common mistakes.

Articles

The words 'a', 'an' and 'the' are called articles. They always come before a noun/noun phrase and help to identify the person, place, animal or thing referred to by them. The articles 'a' and 'an' are called indefinite articles, and they come before singular countable nouns and they identify the person or thing they represent in a general way. For example, in the sentence 'A woman came in a car', the indefinite article 'a' only identifies the nouns that follow as some woman and as some car, without telling us anything more specific about their identity. Similarly, in the sentence 'I saw an object lying there', the indefinite article 'an' simply identifies what was seen as some object—again in a general way. The indefinite article 'a' is used when the following noun begins with a consonant sound, and the indefinite article 'an' appears when the following noun begins with a vowel sound. Look at the use of 'a' and 'an' in the sentences below. The nouns which follow the indefinite article in the first four sentences all begin with consonant sounds—/p/, /k/, /s/ and /l/. In contrast, the nouns following the indefinite article in the last four sentences begin with vowel sounds—/ɑʊ/, /ʌ/, /e/ and /ɪ/.

I wrote with *a* pencil.
Bina was baking *a* cake.
He is *a* singer.
A lion roared.
An owl hooted.
Let me give you *an* umbrella.
Can I have *an* egg, please.
She is *an* Indian.

It is important to remember that we are referring to consonant and vowel *sounds*, and not *letters*. For example, in the sentences below, the indefinite article 'a' appears with words beginning with the letter 'u', because in the words concerned the letter is pronounced as the consonant sound /j/.

Vinod wants to join *a* university.
We are members of *a* union.

Similarly, in the sentences below, the indefinite article 'an' is used before words beginning with the letter 'h', because in the words concerned the consonant letter is silent.

You are *an* honest person.
I have been waiting here for *an* hour.

The article 'the' is the definite article, and it precedes both singular and plural nouns to refer to the person or thing they represent in a specific way. For example in the sentence, 'Deepu saw *the* helicopter take off', the use of the definite article indicates that it was a specific helicopter that Deepu saw, and this information is shared by the speaker as well as by the listener. Again, in the sentence 'Will you watch *the* film?' the use of the definite article indicates a specific film, the identity of which is known by both the speaker and the listener. Look at the following sentences in which the nouns following the definite article are all specific instances of the persons, places, animals or things they represent.

The acrobat ran up *the* rope ladder.
Keep *the* apple and *the* banana on a plate.

The dog chased a cat up a tree.
Hamid was waiting for Alok at *the* bus stop.

It would be useful to remember that the definite article 'the' is pronounced as /ðə/ when it appears before words beginning with a consonant sound, as in: *the* pin, *the* box, *the* fish, *the* shop, etc. It is, however, pronounced as /ðɪ/ when it is used before words beginning with vowel sounds, as in: *the* orange, *the* apple, *the* ulcer, *the* east, etc.

The indefinite article is used in the following situations.

- before a noun that is introduced for the first time in speech or writing

  I will tell you about *an* officer in the Indian navy. (The speaker/reader has not heard of the officer ever before.)

- before a noun which represents not an individual person or thing, but an instance of a whole class

  A doctor must have a lot of compassion. (Here the reference is not to a particular doctor, but to all members of the profession.)

- to indicate the numeral one

  I gave him a rupee. (meaning, one rupee)

- with personal names in two very specific situations
  - when the person referred to is a stranger to the speaker

    Father has gone to the bank with *a* Dr Sen. (The speaker does not know who Dr Sen is.)

  - when the qualities of the person, and not the person herself, are being referred to

    Rohit is turning out to be *an* Einstein. (very good at physics)
    Your niece is *a* Sonal Mansingh. (an exceptionally talented dancer)

The definite article is used in the following situations.

- before a noun that has already been mentioned and is referred to again in the same piece of speech or writing.

  Nimi bought *a* book on marine life. After she read *the* book, she decided to study oceanography.

- when used with a singular countable noun, 'the' is used to refer to a whole class of things, objects, etc.

    The psychiatrist is a doctor who treats mental illness. (referring to all doctors who have specialised in the area)

- when used to refer to a noun which is the only one of its kind in a particular situation

    I would like to speak to *an* employee here. (when there are many employees)
    but I would like to speak to *the* person in charge here. (when there is only one person in charge)

- when the noun following it is made specific by the use of a qualifying word, phrase or clause

    The <u>red</u> flowers are geraniums. (underlined word, an adjective)
    The flowers <u>in the vase</u> are geraniums. (underlined words, an adjectival phrase)
    The flowers <u>that I gave you</u> are geraniums. (underlined words, an adjectival clause)

- before the names of mountain ranges (but not mountain peaks or hills), oceans, seas, rivers, lakes and groups of islands (but not with a single island)

    Mount Everest is the highest peak in *the* Himalayas.
    The Andaman and Nicobar islands and Sri Lanka are both close to India.
    We flew over *the* Pacific Ocean.

- before points on the earth, and before points of the compass, as in, 'the South Pole', 'the equator', 'the west', 'the Middle East', etc.
- with adjectives in the superlative degree

    Susan is *the* fastest sprinter in the college.

- before adjectives when they are used as nouns referring to a class of people, animals, things, etc.

    The strong can carry the logs of wood upstairs. (meaning those who are strong)

- before the names of holy books, as in 'the Gita', 'the Koran', 'the Granth Sahib', etc.
- before the names of well-known buildings, the names of trains and the names of newspapers, as in 'the Rashtrapati Bhavan', 'the Rajdhani Express', 'the Indian Express', etc.
- before the plural forms of proper nouns to refer to families

    The Chackos are wonderful hosts.

- before the singular forms of proper nouns to suggest a comparison

    Anu is *the* Sania Mirza of our college. (implying that she is a brilliant tennis player)

- before names of countries which consist of more than one word

    Roma used to live in *the* United States of America.
    but Roma used to live *in* America.

Articles *are not used* in the following cases.

- usually, before proper nouns, except in the situations given above
- before abstract nouns, e.g., 'peace', and names of activities and subjects of study, e.g., 'gardening' and 'economics', except when they are made specific by some phrases that follow them

    We long for peace. (*not* 'the peace')
    but We long for *the* peace of the hills.

- before mass nouns like 'air' and 'milk' except when these are made specific by a following phrase or clause

    We breathe air. (*not* 'the air')
    but We breathe *the* air in the open.

- before the names of most diseases (exceptions headache/cold)

    Cancer, if detected early, is curable.

- before names of colleges and universities, if the name happens to include 'of'

    Ranjit took a degree in law from *the* University of Hyderabad.

but Ranjit took a degree in law from Delhi University.

- before the names of meals had at different times of the day

  He took us out to dinner.

  but *The* dinner we had at Balu's Tiffin Centre was delicious.

- before nouns like 'church', 'college', 'hospital', when we are referring to them in relation to their primary purpose (prayer, higher education, treatment for illness, etc.) and not as places or buildings

  Her daughter is at college. (for education)

  but Her daughter cycles to *the* college. (the building and surrounding campus)

  They go twice a week to church. (to pray)

  but They reached *the* church before 7 a.m. (the building)

- usually before some collective nouns such as 'humankind', 'society' and 'humanity'

  This is a great service to humanity.

  Will society forget such a great person?

- in phrases with preposition 'by' showing means of transport/transmission

  Mansur came to the city by train.

  You can go by car.

Exercise 1

Fill in the blanks in the sentences below with 'a', 'an' or 'the'. In case more than one can be used, and in case you think one would be more appropriate than the other(s), use it to complete the sentence. If the blank space does not need any of the three words, indicate this with an X.

a. ……….. peacock is in danger of extinction.

b. Could you get me ……….. kilogram of tea, please.

c. There is ……….. European and ……….. Eskimo among the tourists.

d. ……….. Sally I know lives in Bhubaneswar.

e. Sajita found .... wallet on her way home. She took .... wallet to the police station.

f. We must work to save .... tigers from becoming extinct.

g. Have you had .... breakfast?

h. You must reach .... school before 9 a.m.

i. It is .... awe-inspiring sight to see .... Brahmaputra in spate.

j. This is a painting of .... Western Ghats, and that is a photograph of .... Mahabaleshwar peak.

k. Mary will go to .... school when she is three.

l. Our library has three copies of .... Mahabharata.

Exercise 2

Some of the following sentences may have errors relating to the use of articles. Rewrite the sentences correctly.

a. The oranges and lemons are citrus fruits.

b. Asif is going to visit the Oxford University.

c. The elephants and the lions are found in India.

d. Have you been to Nilgiri hills?

e. History is not really Lisa's favourite subject, but she finds the history of the Greeks fascinating.

f. You can take Kerala Express to Shoranur.

g. The children have been sent to the bed.

h. Gold you buy here is of excellent quality.

i. Manoj heard a old tale about an unicorn.

j. Philosophy discussed in this book is very difficult to understand.

Prepositions

Prepositions are words that appear in front of nouns, noun phrases, pronouns and gerunds (*-ing* forms of verbs that behave like nouns) and link them to other nouns, verbs and adjectives in the sentence. The words that follow prepositions are called their objects, and the prepositions are said to govern them. The preposition together with its object forms a prepositional phrase. Look at the examples of prepositions (in italics) which link the underlined words in the sentences below.

He smiled *at* Anju.
verb noun

Prema kept the pen *on* the table.
noun noun phr.

They were good *to* her.
adj. pronoun

Mina is fond *of* reading.
verb gerund

Though a preposition is usually placed before the noun it governs, it can also appear sometimes in other positions. For example:

Dr Siddique is the person I spoke *to*.
What is the documentary *on*?
Gita needed something to wipe the plates *with*.

Simple prepositions consist of one word. Some of these are given below.

about	above	across	after	against	along
among	around	at	before	behind	below
beneath	beside	besides	between	by	despite
down	during	for	from	in	into
inside	of	on	outside	over	round
since	than	through	throughout	till	to
towards	under	until	up	upon	with

Complex or phrase prepositions consist of two or more words. For example:

along with	away from	because of	due to
except for	together with	instead of	in comparison to
in spite of	according to	in view of	up to
but for	next to	on account of	apart from

There are other words that look like adjectives or verbs but they are used as prepositions. These include:

barring concerning excepting following including like minus near plus unlike

Prepositions can have different functions. Thus, they indicate time, place, purpose, direction, movement, means/instrumentality, concession, comparison, source and manner. Look at the following sentences where the prepositions have these functions.

> Sudha sits *between* Saroj and Usman. (position)
> Vijay went *from* Kochi *to* Kottayam. (movement and direction)
> Father returned *at* 6 o'clock. (time)
> The road has been blocked *because of* the wedding procesion. (reason)
> We went to the market *for* vegetables. (purpose)
> Jaya cut the lemon *with* a knife. (instrument)
> Let's go to Mumbai *by* bus. (means)
> *In spite of* the heat, the children are playing outdoors. (concession)
> The bird looks *like* a koel. (comparison)
> Leela does all her work *with* great care. (manner)
> They got water *from* the river. (source)

Exercise 1

Fill in the blanks in the following sentences with suitable prepositions.

a. The bag is .... the top rack .... the cupboard.

b. They are sorry .... having disturbed you.

c. The woman .... the car is my neighbour.

d. Did you see the article .... the applications .... biotechnology?

e. Shikha spent a day .... her aunt .... 12, Begumpet .... Hyderabad.

f. The baby slept peacefully .... the telephone rang.

g. .... the bandh, people went out to work.

h. Rini was angry .... Simon and spoke harshly .... him.

i. The building is deserted .... pigeons and mice.

j. His clients are happy ……….. Mani's work.

Exercise 2

Correct errors in the use of prepositions in the following sentences.

a. Among the two sisters, Habiba is the better dancer.
b. They left in midnight to their village.
c. Manu has been living at Dubai since ten years.
d. The shop is under my flat.
e. The girls sat down besides the lake.
f. There is a reference of the drug in page 33 on chapter 6.
g. We insisted to going out for a walk.
h. Don't interfere with my affairs.
i. He was in great need for affection.
j. I am surprised over the slow pace of life here.

Verbs

Let us look at different types of verbs and see how they are used in English.

Action and non-action verbs

Verbs can be divided into two main classes, which we shall call *action verbs* and *non-action verbs*. (Some grammar books use the names dynamic and stative for these two classes of verbs.) Look at the sentences below.

The boys *are running*.
The goats *are jumping* over the fence.
The peacocks *danced* in the rain.
I *chopped* wood.
Sarala *threw* a pebble into the water.

The italicised verbs above are called action verbs (or 'dynamic verbs') as they indicate some action performed deliberately by a 'doer'. Other examples of action verbs are 'eat', 'walk', 'talk', 'fight', etc.

Compare these with the verbs in the following sentences.

Ahmed *is* sick.
Seeta *looks* tired.

No action is indicated by the verbs 'is' and 'looks' in the above sentences. In other words, there is no action/activity performed. But these verbs indicate a certain condition, or state, and so they are called stative verbs.

Here are some more examples of non-action verbs.

I *think* Hindi is a difficult language.
I *remember* this place well.
I *suppose* they will come.

The verbs 'think', 'remember' and 'suppose' refer to mental activities that go on inside the mind and cannot be seen. We can therefore call them non-action verbs.

Look at some more examples of non-action verbs.

I *see* a bird sitting on that tree.
I *hear* the sound of a gun.
I *feel* an insect crawling over my leg.

'See', 'hear', and 'feel' are called verbs of sensation. They refer to things that we can do with the help of the five senses (sight, hearing, smell, taste, touch). As they do not involve any deliberate action by a doer, we call them non-action verbs. Notice the difference between the verbs in the two pairs of sentences below.

A: *Look* at that bird sitting on the tree.
B: I can't *see* anything.

A: *Listen* to the song.
B: I can't *hear* anything.

'Look' and 'listen ' could be called action verbs, because they refer to actions that are done deliberately. But 'see' and 'hear' do not indicate deliberate actions.

Finally, there is another group of non-action verbs, appearing in the sentences below.

I *have* a house in Bangalore.
He *owns* five cars.
This watch *belongs* to my brother.

'Have', 'own' and 'belong' indicate ownership, but they do not refer to any action.

As we shall explain later, action verbs are used differently from non-action verbs. For example, you can say:

I *am eating* a mango.

But you cannot say:

*I *am seeing* a man on the road.

(Note: When you see an asterisk or 'star' sign [*] in front of a sentence, it tells you that the sentence is incorrect.)

Exercise 1

Pick out the verbs in the sentences below and say whether they are action verbs or non-action verbs.

a. My brothers write books.
b. The boxes contain my clothes.
c. I always hope for the best.
d. I want a glass of milk.
e. He believes in us.
f. The boy turned away from the window.
g. Janet washed the dishes.
h. The chair is comfortable.
i. All the passengers boarded the train.
j. Suma felt happy at the sight of her childhood home.

FINITE AND NON-FINITE VERBS

Look at the following sentences.

Cows *eat* grass.
The boy *eats* idlis every day.
I *ate* some fish yesterday.

The verbs used in these sentences are 'eat', 'eats' and 'ate'. They are called *finite verbs,* or finite forms of a verb, because together with an object noun (present here, but not always necessary) they form the predicates of sentences. In other words, a sentence cannot be complete unless it has a finite verb, whose form changes according to tense, number and person.

Now compare the sentences above with the following sentence.

*The boy *eating* a mango.

This sentence is not complete. Something is missing. Instead, you could say:

The boy *is eating* a mango.

The sentence carries a clear meaning now, but only after we have used the word 'is' along with the verb 'eating'. 'Eating' is called a non-finite verb, or a non-finite form of the verb 'eat'. When used by themselves, non-finite verbs cannot make the predicate of a sentence complete; they have to be used with some other word, such as 'is' in order to convey a complete meaning. 'Is' is called a helping verb or an auxiliary verb, as it 'helps' a non-finite verb to convey a complete meaning.

Here is another example of a non-finite verb.

*The boy *eaten* a mango.

This sentence is also incomplete. You have to use a helping verb together with 'eaten' in order to have a complete sentence. You could say:

The boy *has eaten* a mango.

'Has' is the helping verb in this sentence, which must be used together with the non-finite verb form 'eaten' in order to have a complete sentence. 'Eat', 'eats', 'ate', 'eating' and 'eaten' are different forms of the verb 'eat'. 'Eat', 'eats' and 'ate' are called finite forms, while 'eating' and 'eaten' are non-finite forms.

Certain names are given to the different forms of verbs. 'Eat' is called the stem form, because all the other forms are produced from it. 'Eats' is called the 'stem+*s*' form. You can easily understand why this name is used. The stem form and the stem+*s* form are the simple present tense forms, and 'ate' is the simple the past tense form. 'Eating' is called the 'stem+*ing*' form, or the present participle form. 'Eaten' is the 'stem +*en*' form, or the past participle form.

Exercise 2

Identify the verb forms in the following sentences and say whether they are finite or non-finite. For example, in 'Pratap came home smiling', 'came' is the finite verb in the sentence and 'smiling' is a non-finite verb that functions as an adverb.

a. We picked up the scattered coins.
b. Teresa sat reading in a corner of the room.
c. Vijay stepped on the broken glass pieces and cried in pain.
d. The boy entered the house soaking wet.
e. Trekking is an exciting activity.
f. Omana added boiling water to the tea leaves.
g. Yogesh was happy to go to school.
h. Dentists recommend brushing after every meal.
i. The children longed to eat icecream.
j. Malu gave me a beautifully wrapped present.

Regular and irregular verbs

The simple past tense forms of many verbs are formed by adding *-ed* /*-d* / *-ied* to the stem. For example:

ask – asked
burn – burned
drop – dropped
talk – talked
cry – cried
dance – danced
bury – buried
carry – carried

Such verbs are known as regular verbs.

But in many cases, the past tense form of the verb is very different from its stem form. For example:

see – saw
run – ran
buy – bought
get – got
break– broke
make – made

Such verbs are called irregular verbs.

It is easy to remember the past tense forms of regular verbs since all that you have to do is to add *-ed* (or *-d* or *-ied*) to the stem. But in the case of irregular verbs, you have to remember the past tense form of each verb separately; there is no simple rule to help you. Most good dictionaries of English give you the past tense as well as the past participle forms of irregular verbs. For example:

stem	**past tense form**	**participle form**
eat	ate	eaten
see	saw	seen
break	broke	broken
get	got	got

Exercise 3

Look at the verbs in the following sentences and say whether they are regular or irregular.

a. I won a set of twelve coffee mugs at the fair.
b. The trees swayed in the wind.
c. We fried the potatoes with the brinjals.
d. My uncle smiled gently.
e. Nidhi looked surprised.
f. It rained hard in the afternoon.
g. The balloon burst with a loud bang.
h. The police found a bag of fake currency notes in the room.
i. I forgot my doctor's telephone number.

j. The lake froze last winter.

TRANSITIVE AND INTRANSITIVE VERBS

Compare the following sentences.

Ram *laughed*.
*Ram *saw*.

The first sentence is a complete sentence, but the second one is incomplete. On hearing this sentence, one is likely to ask 'What (or whom) did Ram see?' The sentence needs at least one more word, as in the following sentence, in order to be complete.

Ram *saw* a tiger.

The word 'tiger' which follows the verb 'saw' in the above sentence is a noun, and it answers the question 'What did Ram see?' The noun which follows a verb and answers the question 'What?' or 'Whom?' is the object of the verb. A verb which must be followed by an object is called a *transitive verb.* 'See' is thus a transitive verb in the above sentence. Look at other examples of transitive verbs in the sentences below.

Sujit *met* the doctor.
They *are wearing* jackets.
Mridu *tasted* the cake.
You *have learnt* Tamil.
Rani *heard* a whistle.

However, the verb 'laugh', in 'Ram laughed' does not need an object. (You cannot ask 'What did Ram laugh ?' or 'Whom did Ram laugh?') A verb which does not need an object is called an *intransitive verb.* 'Laugh' is an intransitive verb just as the verbs in the sentences below are.

The plane *landed* safely.
The baby *slept*.
The plants *wilted*.
Manoj *shouted* in excitement.
We *live* next door.

Many English verbs are *transitive as well as intransitive.* That is, they are sometimes followed by an object, but they can also be used without an object. For example:

> The mug fell off the table and *broke.*
> He *broke* the mug.

In the first sentence, the verb 'broke' is intransitive, whereas in the second sentence it is transitive. Look at some more examples below.

> My sari caught on a nail and *tore.*
> She *tore* the sheet of paper into two.

> The bell *rang.*
> Shirin *rang* the bell.

> The door *opened.*
> Vivek *opened* the door.

A good learner's dictionary should tell you whether a verb is transitive or intransitive—or whether it is both transitive and intransitive.

Exercise 4

Look at the verbs in the following sentences and say whether they are transitive or intransitive.

a. The patient screamed in pain.

b. The jug broke into many pieces.

c. Lal sat down on the stool.

d. Somebody broke my new pen.

e. Fatima told us a story.

f. The dog was sleeping in its kennel.

g. The ladder bent under his weight.

h. We jumped into the pool.

i. Don't use the scale.

j. Lily listened to the music.

Objects and Complements

Consider the sentence 'Mohan *wrote* a book'. In the sentence, the verb ('wrote') is followed by a noun 'book', which answers the question 'What did Mohan write?'. As explained in the previous section, a noun which follows a verb and answers the question 'What ?' is called the object of the verb, and a verb which takes an object is said to be transitive. Thus, in the sentence above, 'book' is the object of the verb 'wrote', which is a transitive verb. Some verbs take two objects—a direct object and an indirect object. The direct object refers to the person or thing affected by the action of the verb. The indirect object, on the other hand, refers to the person who 'benefits' from the action indicated by the verb. Thus, in the sentence 'Uma gave Susan a scarf', 'a scarf' is the direct object, and 'Susan' is the indirect object. Look at more examples of direct and indirect objects in the sentences below.

I sent him (I Obj) a present (D Obj).
Father will buy Sindhu (I Obj) a bag (D Obj).
Davis got us (I Obj) a pup (D Obj).

The indirect object usually follows the verb, and the direct object comes after the indirect object. However, if the speaker wishes to put the direct object first, then the preposition 'to' or 'for' has to appear in front of the indirect object, as illustrated by the sentences below.

I sent a present *to* him.
Father will buy a bag *for* Sindhu.
Davis got a pup *for* us.

Now look at the sentence 'Mohan became a poet.' Here the verb ('became') is followed by a noun ('poet') which also answers the question 'What did Mohan become?' But we cannot say that the noun 'poet' is the *object* of the verb 'become' because the noun does not represent a person or thing that is separate from it. Instead, we call it the 'complement', which tells us something about the subject. 'Become' is an intransitive verb, which does not take an object, but can take a complement.

What is the difference between an object and a complement? The object refers to a person or thing which is different from the subject. In the sentence 'Mohan wrote a book', the object ('book') refers to a thing which is different from the subject ('Mohan'). But in the sentence 'Mohan became a poet', the word 'poet' refers to Mohan, who is the subject of the sentence. That is why 'poet' is the complement of the verb in the sentence, and not its object.

Exercise 5

Look at the underlined word(s) in the following sentences and say whether they are the direct or the indirect objects of the italicised verbs.

a. She *is* a nurse.
b. He *threw* the ball up in the air.
c. Kanchan *is sleeping* in her room.
d. Please *switch off* the lights.
e. Jagdish *shut* the door.
f. Anju *walked* slowly to thc market.
g. The boy *gave* a chocolate to him.
h. My father *teaches* geography.
i. Vyasa *wrote* the Mahabharata.
j. The water *flowed* down the hill.
k. The boy in the blue shirt *was* my neighbour.
l. We *bought* father a kurta.

Tenses

TIME AND TENSE

The word 'tense' refers to the different forms of a verb which tell us when the action referred to happens—before, at the time of or after the moment of speech. There are two main tenses in English: the present tense and the past tense. Each of these is divided into a number of sub-tenses. The complete system of tenses is as follows.

- simple present
- present progressive (or present continuous)
- present perfect
- present perfect progressive
- simple past
- past progressive (or continuous)
- past perfect
- past perfect progressive

It is important to note that English has no future tense. Many grammar books tell us that there are three tenses English: present tense, past tense and future tense. This is not true for there is no future tense in English. Why do we say this? We have explained above that the word 'tense' refers to the changing forms of the verb which tell us when an action is performed or when an event happens in relation to the moment when the speaker (or writer) utters (or writes) the sentence. In English, verbs have two different tense forms that indicate whether something occurs in the present or in the past. For example:

> We *go* to school every day. (present tense form of 'go', indicating an action taking place at the present time)
> We *went* to school yesterday. (past tense form of 'go', indicating action in the past)

But if we want to talk about an action that is expected to take place in the future, there is no separate 'tense', or form of the verb, that can be used. For example:

> He *will go* to school tomorrow.

Although there are several different ways of indicating future action in English, we do not make use of any special 'tense' for this purpose. We use some other means instead. Therefore, instead of talking about the 'future tense', we will refer to the 'different ways of showing future action'. These are listed below.

a. future action shown by 'will' or 'shall', together with the simple present tense form of the main verb

b. future action shown by 'going to'
c. future action shown by the use of the present progressive tense
d. future action shown by the use of the simple present tense

Each of these will be described in detail later.

PRESENT TENSE

Present tense forms in English are of four kinds.

The simple present

In the simple present tense, the verb is used in the stem form if the subject is plural, and in the stem+*s* form if the subject is singular. For example:

> We *eat* rice. (stem)
> Ashok *eats* rice. (stem + *s*)
> They *love* chocolates. (stem)
> She *loves* chocolates. (stem + *s*)

Uses of the simple present

- The simple present tense is used to refer to eternal truths (things that are always true or believed to be true). For example:

  > The sun *rises* in the east.
  > Hydrogen *is* lighter than air.
  > Arteries *carry* blood from the heart to different parts of the body.
  > Hard work *leads* to success.

Exercise 1

Fill in the blanks in the sentences below, using verbs in the simple present form to express eternal truths.

a. Most snakes .... (lay) eggs, but the python .... (give) birth to young ones.

b. People who .... (work) for long hours in the sun often .... (get) sun burnt.

c. Computers .... (store) large amounts of data.
d. Magnets .... (attract) iron filings.
e. Plants .... (produce) their own food through the process of photosynthesis. During this process, plants .... (take in) carbon-dioxide from the air and .... (give out) oxygen.
f. Our lungs .... (expand) when we .... (breathe in) and .... (contract) when we .... (breathe out). The lungs .... (have) tiny blood vessels which are called capillaries. Oxygen .... (go) directly into the blood through these capillaries. The heart .... (pump) blood to different parts of the body.

- The simple present tense is also used to refer to 'present truths' (things that are true at the present time but may not be true in the future). For example:

  Kochi *is* the business capital of Kerala.
  My brother *works* in a rubber factory.
  Ravi *stays* with his uncle and aunt.

Exercise 2

Fill in the blank spaces in the sentences below, using verbs in the simple present tense to show present truths.

Raghavan .... (live) in Kochi. He .... (work) in a bank. He .... (have) two children, who .... (go) to an English medium school. Raghavan's wife .... (teach) Sanskrit in the school. His brother .... (be) an artist. He .... (paint) pictures.

- Next, the simple present tense is used to refer to routine or habitual activity (actions that are performed regularly, or every day). For example:

  Hari *gets up* at 6.00 a.m. He *brushes* his teeth and *drinks* a glass of milk. Then he *takes* a bath and *puts on* his school uniform. He *leaves* the house at 7.00 a.m. and *waits* outside his house for the school bus. After lessons, he *plays* football or cricket with other children. He *returns* home at 4.30 p.m., *takes off* his uniform and *goes out* again to play with his friends.

Exercise 3

Describe a typical day in the life of some member of your family. Describe some things that he/she does every day as routine activities.

- Further, the simple present tense is used to describe objects, places, people, etc. For example:

  A pressure-cooker *is* a metal vessel with a tight-fitting lid, through which steam cannot escape. The lid *has* a tiny opening, called a vent, over which a valve *sits*. Pressure cookers *help* us to cook food quickly.

  The new Maruti-Suzuki Swift *has* a 4-cylinder, 1300 cc engine which *produces* 83 bhp. It *has* independent suspension on all four wheels and *runs* 14 kilometres on a litre of petrol. The car *costs* Rs 4.2 lakh in Tiruvananthapuram.

  The thief, who was arrested by the police, *is* about 165 cm in height. He *has* large eyes and brown hair and he *weighs* about 75 kg. There *is* a long scar on the left side of his face.

Exercise 4

Write the following descriptions in three sentences each, using verbs in the simple present form where required.

a. The house in which you live

b. Your best friend

c. A mobile phone

d. The college garden

e. Your grandmother

- The simple present tense is also used to describe or to demonstrate an action or activity which is in progress ('going on') at the present time. For example:

  Shoaib Akhtar *bowls*. Tendulkar *hits* the ball towards the square leg boundary.

Here, the simple present tense is used to talk about an action which is actually in progress at the moment of speaking. (You can see that the examples are taken from a running commentary on a cricket match. However, we use the present progressive tense more often for this purpose.) You can also see this on television, for example, when an expert teaches the viewers how to cook a dish. For example:

> Today, I will show you how to make fish curry. First, I *chop* some onions and *fry* them in oil until they are brown. Then, I *add* some curry powder to the onions and *heat* the mixture over a low flame. Then I *put in* . . .

Exercise 5

Imagine that you are giving a cookery demonstration on television. Tell your viewers about the different actions you perform while preparing a typical Kerala dish. Use the simple present tense as shown above.

- Finally, the simple present tense is used in newspaper headlines to make a news report more dramatic. For example:

  Minister *says* 'Sorry!'
  Indian *wins* international award
  Sick unit *shuts* down

Exercise 6

Write headlines for the following news reports. The headline should not have more than five words and should include a verb in the simple present form.

a. The Indian under-19 cricket team defeated the Sri Lankan team by six wickets in the Arjun Ranatunga Trophy match which was played in

Colombo yesterday. The captain of the Indian team said every player in the team had contributed to this victory.

b. On Thursday, the chief minister of Kerala inaugurated a new computer training centre in Kottayam. In his inaugural speech, the chief minister said that this centre would provide advanced training in software development, and would open up new job opportunities for the youth of Kerala.

The present progressive tense

In the present progressive tense, the verb is used in the progressive (stem + *ing*) form and some form of the verb 'be' (*is, am, are*) is used in front of the verb, as a helping verb or auxiliary. For example:

> My father *is playing* a game of chess.
> My friends *are walking* to the post office.

Uses of the present progressive

- The present progressive tense is used to refer to an action which is in progress at the moment of speaking. It is often used during running sports commentaries on radio or television, when a commentator who is watching the match has to describe to his audience the actions that are taking place while he speaks. For example:

  The two Pakistani opening batsmen *are going out* to start the innings. The Indian fielders *are taking up* their positions. The bowler *is getting ready* to bowl the first ball. He *is walking back* for the start of his run.

Exercise 7

Fill in the blanks in the dialogues below, using the present progressive tense.

a. Teacher : Ravi, what are you doing?

   Ravi : I .... a story book, ma'am.

   Teacher : Do you think you should be doing that now when your classmates .... (make) their presentations?

b. Mother : Seema, the telephone .... (ring). Will you answer it?

Seema : I am sorry, but I can't, Mother. I .... (take) a bath.

- The present progressive tense is also used to show that an activity is only temporary and is not expected to continue for a long time. Here is an example.

Raghu *is teaching* art in a school in Mangalore.

Here, the use of the present progressive does not necessarily indicate action in progress at the moment of speaking. Raghu may not actually be inside a classroom, teaching students, when this sentence is spoken. Compare the two sentences below.

Raghu *teaches* art in a school in Mangalore. (simple present)
Raghu *is teaching* art in a school in Mangalore. (present progressive)

The use of the simple present in the first sentence indicates that teaching art is Raghu's permanent profession. On the other hand, the present progressive suggests that Raghu has taken up the job only temporarily, and is doing it during the present period of time. Here is another example.

Raghu *teaches* mathematics, but this year he *is teaching* geography.

In the sentence above, we see a contrast between a long-term activity and a more short-term one.

- The present progressive is sometimes used to indicate action in the future. Here is an example.

I *am starting* a new business next year.

As mentioned earlier, there are several different ways of indicating future activity, and using the present progressive is one of them. It has a rather special meaning, which we shall examine later, when we talk about the different ways of referring to future activity.

Exercise 8

Fill in the blanks in the paragraphs below, using the present progressive tense forms of the verbs in brackets.

a. My uncle, who lives in Varanasi, ... (visit) Kerala. He .... (spend) a week in a village near Guruvayoor. He .... (travel) all over the state by bus, although it is his first trip to the place.

b. Mohanan fell ill and went to see a doctor, who advised him to be careful about his diet and to take plenty of exercise. So now Mohanan .... (drink) a litre of milk every day. He .... (eat) plenty of fruit and .... (go) for a walk in the park every morning.

c. The president of India .... (arrive) in Kolkata next week. Everyone is busy preparing for his visit. Workers .... (clean up) the streets. Painters .... (paint) the buildings.

d. I live in Chennai, where the coffee is excellent. But I .... (spend) a week in Delhi. I can't get filter coffee here, so I .... (drink) tea instead. I .... (eat) chapatis instead of idlis and quite like the change.

e. The Republic Day parade has begun. The soldiers .... (march) into the stadium. The president .... (take) the salute and all the other guests .... (stand up) to honour the national flag. The military band .... (play) the national anthem.

Note that not all verbs appear in the present prograssive form. We have already mentioned that verbs can be divided into two classes, to which we gave the names action and non-action verbs. One important difference between them is that non-action verbs are generally not used in the simple progressive tense, except in special cases. Using these verbs in the present progressive tense leads to some common mistakes, such as the following.

*He *is having* five horses.

*The food *is smelling* good.

*I *am seeing* many people on the road.

*I *am remembering* the house in which I was born

*She *is knowing* the answer to this question.

*He *is not believing* your statement.

*I *am feeling* cold.

*I *am thinking* you are very wise.

Sometimes, we do find non-action verbs being used in the present progressive form in special cases. Here are some examples.

She *is having* dinner.
He *is having* a haircut.
They *are having* a party.
She *is having* a great time.
My sister *is having* a baby.

These are, however, not exceptions to what we said earlier for 'have' in the above sentences is not used in its primary sense of 'own' or 'possess'. In the above sentences, it means 'eating dinner', 'getting a haircut', 'arranging a party', 'enjoying' and 'expecting a baby'. Similarly, 'see' and 'feel' are used in the present progressive tense—when they are used to indicate what is not their primary meaning.

I *am seeing* my friend this evening. (meeting my friend)
The doctor *is feeling* the patient's pulse. (to touch with the fingers to check something)

Exercise 9

Fill in the blanks in the sentences below by using either the simple present or the present progressive form of the verb given in brackets.

A meeting of the students is in progress. The secretary of the Students' Union .... (speak). He .... (read out) the annual report of the union. He .... (think) that the college should organise a debate and offer a prize to the best speaker, as the union .... (have) a lot of money. But some of the other students .... (feel) that the money should be used to help deserving students with their fees and books.

The present perfect tense

In the present perfect tense, the verb is used in the past participle form, while either 'have' or 'has' is used in front of it as a helping verb. For example:

The child *has eaten* a biscuit.
The boys *have gone* to school.
We *have left* the clothes in your room.
Lekha *has come* home.
You *have not done* your work.
I *have given away* all the books.

Uses of the present perfect tense

The use of the present perfect tense shows that an action was completed sometime in the past and, further, that the completed action has some kind of relevance to the present moment of speech. (The word 'perfect' tells us that the action is complete.) The present perfect tense is thus the opposite of the present progressive, which is used to show that an action is not complete but is still in progress at the time of speaking. The example below shows this contrast between the present progressive and the present perfect.

Mother : Usha, what are you doing?
Usha : I *am doing* my homework, Mother. (present progressive)
(Half an hour later)
Mother : Usha, are you still doing your homework?
Usha : No, Mother. I *have done* it. (present perfect)

The present perfect tense does not tell us when an action was performed. Strictly speaking, it has no time reference. For example:

He *has read* 'Chemmeen'.

We are not told when the action of reading the book was performed. But we can guess that it was performed sometime in the past. Look at another example.

I *have been* to New York.

Again, we are not told when the speaker went to New York but we understand that it must have been sometime in the past. However, what is suggested is that although the action was performed in the past, its effect remains at the present time.

He *has read* 'Chemmeen' (and he remembers the story clearly).

I *have been* to New York (and I can recommend a hotel there, for example).

I *have cleaned* the table. (It is clean now.)

Exercise 10

a. Fill in the blanks in the sentences below, using the present perfect tense.

Mother : Rima, are you ready to go to school?

Rima : Yes, mother. I .... (brush) my teeth. I .... (comb) my hair. I .... (pack) my books in my school bag.

Mother : What about your breakfast?

Rima : I .... (eat) my breakfast already.

Mother : Good girl! Well, your bus .... (come). Bye, Rima.

Rima : Bye, Mother!

b. The following scene takes place in a school. An inspection team is to visit the school on the next day and everyone is busy cleaning the place. The headmaster is questioning one of the students to find out how much work has been done. Fill in the blanks in the dialogue, using the given verbs in the present perfect tense.

Headmaster : Are the classrooms clean?

Student : Yes sir, we .... (wash) the floors with water.

Headmaster : What about the furniture?

Student : We .... (wipe) all the desks and benches. There is no dust on them.

Headmaster : And the banners? Are they in place?

Student : Yes sir. We .... (put up) the banners on the walls.

Headmaster : What about the invitations?

Studen : We .... (send out) all the invitations to guests as well as to parents.

Headmaster : Good. Is someone going to take photographs?

Student : Yes sir. We .... (arrange for) a photographer.

Headmaster : Excellent. You seem to have done a good job.

Student : Thank you, sir.

The present perfect progressive tense

The present perfect progressive tense is, as the name suggests, a combination of the present perfect and the present progressive tenses, in form as well as in meaning. Here is an example.

Sheila *has been teaching* in this school since 25 July 2004.

Notice that the verb ('teach') is in the *-ing* form used in the progressive tense, but there are two helping verbs that come before it. The first is a form of 'have' ('have'/ 'has'), followed by 'been', which is the past participle form of 'be'. The presence of the progressive form ('teaching') suggests action in progress, while the presence of the participle ('has been') suggests completed action. The combination of the present progressive and the present perfect tenses tells us that:

a. the action began at some point in the past (25 July 2004);
b. the action has continued without a break until the present moment (the moment of speaking).

Here are some more examples.

Mahesh *has been playing* tennis for the last two hours and he is tired.

The boys *have been waiting* to see the principal since 7.00 a.m.

In the first sentence, Mahesh started playing tennis two hours ago and is playing even at the present moment. In the second sentence too, the wait began in the past and continues into the present.

The prepositions 'since' and 'for' are often used with verbs in the present perfect progressive tense. 'Since' is used to refer to the point of time (in the past) at which an action began, while 'for' refers to the period of time during which the action has been in progress. For example:

I *have been living* in Delhi since 1988.

I *have been living* in Delhi for 18 years.

The present perfect progressive is used to highlight the continuity of an action. In both the sentences above, the speaker wants to convey that there has been no break or interruption in the act of 'living' in Delhi. Note that 'since' cannot be used to indicate a period of time. Mistakes of the following type are thus very common.

*He *has been teaching* since fourteen years.

Finally, note the difference between 'He *is playing* tennis' (present progressive) and 'He *has been playing* tennis' (present perfect progressive). The present progressive tells us that the action is in progress now; it says nothing about when the action began. The present perfect progressive, on the other hand, indicates that the action began in the past and has continued until the present time.

Exercise 11

Fill in the blanks in the sentences below, using the given verbs in the simple present, present progressive, present perfect or present perfect progressive tenses, as required.

a. My brother is a writer. He .... (write) novels. He .... (write) novels since 1990 and .... (write) 15 novels so far.

b. I love learning languages. I .... (learn) different languages since I was in school. So far, I .... (learn) eight languages. I .... (learn) Japanese now.

c. Rajeev : Where do you live, Babu?

Babu : I .... (live) in Thrissur.

Rajeev : Thrissur? I thought you were from Kochi.

Mohanan : Yes, I was born in Kochi, but I .... (move) to Thrissur now.

I .... (be) there since 1999 and I .... (build) a house there.

Rajeev : Do you work in Thrissur?

Babu : Yes, I .... (teach) in a school there. My wife .... (work) there too, but this year she .... (do) a teacher training course in Hyderabad. Her school .... (give) her a year's leave.

Rajeev : Does she write to you?

Mohanan : Oh yes, she .... (write) to me regularly. She also .... (talk) to the children on the telephone every night. She .... (miss) them very much.

Past Tense

In English, there are four different forms of the verb referring to action in the past.

The simple past

The simple past tense takes the stem + *ed* form in regular verbs. For example: *ask, asked; reach, reached; pray, prayed; smile, smiled,* etc. With irregular verbs, the simple past form is completely different from the stem form, e.g., *break, broke; sit, sat,* etc.

Uses of the simple past tense

- The simple past tense is used to refer to an action, activity or event that took place sometime in the past—that is, before the moment of speaking. The reference to past time is commonly (but not always) shown by time adverbs. For example:

  He *played* in the match yesterday.
  She *drove* to Mumbai last week.
  The trees *shook* violently in the strong wind.
  Water *flowed* down the slope.
  Verghese *enrolled* for a course in spoken English.

Exercise 12

a. Fill in the blanks using the past tense forms of the verbs in brackets.

i. Kalidas .... (be) a great poet. He .... (live) 2000 years ago.

ii. We ………… (have) a house in Alapuzha but we ………… (sell) it last year.

iii. The child ………… (break) the cup. He ………… (be) sleepy and he ………… (drop) the cup on the floor.

b. Fill in the blanks using verbs in either the simple past or present perfect tense, as required.

i. Madan first ………… (visit) Nagaland in 1980, when he ………… (be) only 15 years old. He ………… (fall) in love with the place at once. Later, he ………… (return) to Nagaland many times, and ………… (become) an expert on it.

ii. My brother is a famous artist. He ………… (paint) many beautiful pictures, but his most famous painting is a portrait of Indira Gandhi, which he ………… (paint) in 1980.

- Generally, the simple past tense indicates a single action or activity. For example:

  The postman *delivered* my appointment letter this morning.

  However, it can also be used to indicate habitual activity or to refer to some activity that happened regularly or repeatedly in the past. For example:

  James *played* cricket when he was in school.
  I *walked* to school every morning when I was a child.

  We often use the expression 'used to' to refer to habitual activity in the past. For example:

  I *used to swim* in the sea when I lived in Tiruvananthapuram.

  Notice that 'used to' is followed by the stem form of the verb ('swim') and that it indicates that an activity which was performed regularly in the past is no longer performed at the present time. For example:

  As a young man, I *used to run* 10 kilometres every morning.

'Would' is also used to show habitual activity in the past. For example:

My mother *would* make porridge for our breakfast everyday.

Exercise 13

Fill in the blanks in the sentences below, using the simple past or 'used to' or 'would' to show habitual activity in the past.

Raman .... (live) in Chennai for 10 years. He .... (work) in a bank. He .... (go) to the office at 9.00 every morning and return late at night. He .... (take) his family to the beach every Sunday.

Both the simple past and the present perfect tenses refer to some action that was performed in the past. However, there is an important difference between them. The use of the simple past shows that the speaker merely thinks of the action as being completed. The use of the present perfect, on the other hand, tells us that the effect of the past action is felt at the present time. For example:

He *read* the book in 1986. (simple past)

He *has read* the book and can talk to us about it. (present perfect)

Because the focus of the present perfect tense is not on *when* an action happened in the past, but on its effect in the present, the present perfect is very commonly used without any adverb of time. For example:

I *have seen* this film.

The time at which the action was performed in the past in not mentioned. But if an adverb showing past time is used, we can no longer use the present perfect but only the simple past. Thus, we cannot say:

*I *have seen* this film last year.

The present perfect can only be used with adverbs showing present time. For example:

I *have seen* thirty films this year.

The past progressive tense

In the past progressive tense, the progressive (*-ing*) form of the verb is used together with 'was' or 'were' (past tense forms of 'be'). For example:

> I *was reading* a book at 9.00 p.m. last night.
> My brothers *were playing* cards when the fight started.

Uses of the past progressive tense

- The past progressive tense is used to show that an action was in progress at some time in the past, but is not in progress at the present time. Imagine the following situation. A locked flat is burgled at 8.30 p.m. on a Friday, and the police suspect a person. The next day, Saturday, a police inspector questions him.

  Inspector : What *were you doing* at 8.30 last night?
  Man : Sir, I *was watching* a television serial with my friend at his house.

  Notice the forms of the verbs used by the inspector as well as by the man ('were doing' and 'was watching' respectively). Here the auxiliary verb 'was'/'were', which is in the past tense, is followed by a verb in the participle form ('doing', 'watching'), which shows action in progress. Together, these two indicate action in progress in the past.
- The past progressive is often used to show the overlap in time of two or more actions, both of which were performed in the past. For example:

  > I *was eating* an apple when my friend telephoned.

Here we are told that one action was in progress in the past when a second action took place.

- Sometimes two verbs, both in the past progressive tense, are used for two different actions that were in progress together, at some time in the past. For example:

  > At 9.00 last night, I *was reading* a book while my cousin *was cooking* some rice.

- The past progressive is used to emphasise the duration of some action in the past—to highlight the fact that the action went on for some length of time. Compare the two sentences below.

  It *was raining* yesterday.
  It *rained* yesterday.

The use of the past progressive suggests that the rain lasted for some time. But the use of the simple past only states that it rained.

Exercise 14

Fill in the blanks, using the given verbs in their simple past or past progressive forms.

a. Last night, while my friend .... (take) a walk in the park, he .... (see) a snake. It .... (crawl) through the grass.

b. The bell .... (ring) while I .... (have) a bath. I .... (open) the door and .... (find) a child sitting on the verandah. He .... (read) a comic.

c. When the principal .... (walk) into the classroom, he .... (see) the teacher correcting test papers. The students .... (play) football outside.

The past perfect tense

Look at the sentence below.

> When I *met* my friend in the canteen yesterday, he *had eaten* his lunch already.

This sentence contains two verbs, referring to two different actions, both of which took place in the past. The first verb is in the simple past tense ('met'), while the second is in the past perfect tense ('had eaten'). In the past perfect tense (as in the present perfect tense), the main verb is used in the participle form ('eaten'). But here the helping verb is 'had' (the past tense form of 'have').

Uses of the past perfect tense

The past perfect tense is used to show a sequence of events in the past. If we are talking about a number of events, all of which took place in the past, we may want to indicate which event took place earlier and which one later. The use of the past perfect tense to refer to an event tells us that it took place before another event. The simple past tense is used to refer to the event which took place at a later time in the past. Here is another example.

After I *had read* the newspaper, I tidied the room.

The adverb 'after' clearly tells us that the reading of the newspaper took place earlier than the other action (tidying the room). The same information is emphasised by the use of the past perfect tense to refer to the action that took place earlier. In fact, if the past perfect tense is used in such a situation, it is not necessary to use the adverb 'after'. For example:

When I *had read* the newspaper, I tidied the room.

In the sentence given above, it is quite clear that the action of reading the newspaper took place earlier than that of tidying the room.

Compare the two sentences below.

When I *arrived* at the office yesterday, the meeting *began*.

When I *arrived* at the office yesterday, the meeting *had begun*.

The first sentence suggests that the two actions may have happened simultaneously, at the same time, while the second clearly tells us that one action happened earlier than the other.

Note that the past perfect cannot be used if we are referring to only one action or event in the past. We cannot say:

*I *had met* my friend yesterday.

There must be at least two actions, taking place at different times in the past.

I *had* spoken to my friend before I *wrote* to you.

The adverbs 'before' and 'after' are commonly found in sentences which contain a verb in the past perfect tense. For example:

He *had locked* the front door *before* he *went* to bed.

He *went* to bed *after* he *had locked* the front door.

In sentences such as 'By the time we reached the station, the train had arrived', the verb in the *by the time*-clause, 'reach', represents the action that happened at a later point in time in the past than the action represented by the verb 'arrive' in the main clause. The verb representing the action earlier in time always appears in the past perfect tense while the verb representing the later action appears in the simple past tense. You can look at more examples of this below. In each of the sentences, the verb appearing in the past perfect tense represents the action that happened earlier.

> Father *had made* himself a sandwich by the time I *cooked* lunch.
> By the time the fire engines *came*, we *had put out* the fire.
> By the time Urmila *got* dressed, everybody *had left* for the cinema.
> The children *had slept* by the time the show *began*.

Exercise 15

Fill in the blanks in the sentences below, putting the verbs in brackets in either the simple past or the past perfect tense, as required.

a. The sun .... (set) by the time we .... (leave) for home.

b. I .... (see) the Charminar earlier and .... (go) only to keep Gopi happy.

c. Abu just .... (post) the letter that he .... (write) two weeks ago.

d. Before we .... (get) to the bridge, the water .... (risen) above the danger mark.

e. By the time they .... (consult) a doctor, the man's condition .... (worsen).

The past perfect progressive tense

Look at the following example.

> Yesterday, while I was writing a letter, my friend telephoned from Chennai. He told me that he *had been trying* to contact me for the past two days.

The verb 'had been trying' is in the past perfect progressive tense, which is used to show that an action which began in the past continued up to a certain time, also in the past. Notice that here the present participle form ('trying') is used together with the helping verbs 'had+been'. Compare the two sentences given below.

Arjun *was reading* when Tanvi rang the bell.
Arjun *had been reading* when Tanvi rang the bell.

In the first sentence, the use of the past progressive tense indicates simply that one action was ongoing when a second one happened at some point in the past. The use of the past perfect progressive in the second sentence, however, indicates that the first action had been in progress for a period, continuing up to the time when the second action was performed. Look at the following sentences for more examples of the past perfect progressive tense.

I switched off the over-heated engine, which *had been running* for six hours.
It *had been raining* since three in the morning, and the plane could not take off.
The country's economy *had been improving* steadily until last year's drought.
The coach could see that the swimmer *had been practising*.

Exercise 16

Fill in the blanks in the sentences below, using appropriate tense forms of the verbs in brackets.

a. My father is an engineer. He ……….. (build) houses. He ………… (build) houses for more than 20 years now and ……….. (build) about 200 houses during this time. But now he ……….. (plan) to change his profession. For the last two years, his friends ……….. (ask) him to take up singing as a career. He ……….. (sing) well and …….. (do) several shows. Before he ……….. (become) an engineer, he ………… (dream) of becoming a singer. Father ………… (hope) to succeed in achieving his heart's desire soon.

b. Interviewer : Mr Menon, what do you do?

Menon : I .... (be) a teacher, sir.

Interviewer : How long have you been teaching, Mr Menon?

Menon : I .... (teach) for the last 12 years.

Interviewer : What subjects do you teach?

Menon : I usually .... (teach) chemistry, but I .... (teach) biology this year.

Interviewer : Why?

Menon : Our biology teacher, Ms Monipally, ... (be) away.

She .... (expect) a baby, and .... (be) on leave since February. The principal .... (ask)me to take her classes when she .... (go) on leave.

Interviewer : Is your wife a teacher too, Mr Menon?

Menon : No sir, she .... (be) a nurse.

Interviewer : Does she work in a government hospital?

Menon : She .... (be) in a government hospital last year but at present she .... (work) in a private clinic.

Interviewer : Do you have any experience of working in a foreign country?

Menon : Yes sir, I .... (work) in Kuwait. I .... (be) there from 1999 to 2004.

Interviewer : Would you like to go back there?

Menon : Not at all. As a matter of fact, I .... (get) offers from several employment agencies in Kuwait, but I .... not .... (accept) anything so far.

Reference to future time

- One way of marking future activity is by using 'will' or 'shall', together with the stem form of a verb. Look at the following example.

The match *will begin* at 9.30 tomorrow morning.
I *shall write* to him next week.

Many grammar books tell us that 'will' and 'shall' carry different meanings, but in modern English there is little difference between the two. Both 'will' and 'shall' are frequently contracted, or shortened, (as in, 'I'll', 'they'll') specially while speaking. The sentences above would be spoken as:

The match*'ll* begin at 9.30 tomorrow morning.
I*'ll* write to him next week.

It is difficult to say whether the speaker is using 'will' or 'shall' in these sentences. However, 'shall' is more commonly used with the first person pronouns 'I' and 'we', while 'will' is more commonly used with 'you' (second person) or 'he/she' (third person).

The use of 'will' or 'shall' shows simply that an event or action is expected to happen in the future. No other meaning of any kind is conveyed. But as we shall see, several other kinds of meaning can be conveyed, along with the idea of futurity when we use other ways of referring to future action.

- Reference to future time is also indicated by using 'be + going to' together with the stem form of a verb. For example:

I *am going to buy* a new scooter next week.

Note that in this sentence 'going to' does not indicate physical movement. There is a difference between 'I am going to Malappuram tomorrow' (where 'going to' indicates physical movement) and 'I am going to write a book next year.' The use of 'going to' shows that someone intends to do something in the future or that a future action has been planned by someone. For example:

Soman *is going to join* a new company next year.

This sentence would mean that the doer, Soman, intends or plans to perform a certain action in the future. (The use of 'will' or 'shall', on the other hand, does not show any intention or plan on the part of the doer of the action.) Further, note the difference between the following sentences.

Anju *is going to study* law .
Anju *will study* law.

'Going to' suggests that there is a *definite plan* of Anju's studying law. But when we say 'Anju will study law', we are merely saying that something (here, Anju's studying law) is expected to take place in the future. In the case of the second sentence, we are saying nothing about any definite plan.

The use of 'going to' could also suggest that there is enough reason or evidence to believe that a certain event will take place in the future. For example:

It *is going to* rain tonight. (There are dark clouds in the sky.)

The presence of dark clouds gives us reason to be certain about rain. Look at another example.

Sunil *is going to* fail this test. (He hasn't prepared for the test at all.)

In contrast, the use of 'will' or 'shall' does not carry this meaning. Compare the following sentences.

Our team *is going to* lose this match.
Our team *will lose* this match.

'Going to' conveys a greater feeling of certainty. (The speaker has good reason to believe that his team will lose. The players may have performed so badly that defeat is likely.) In contrast, the use of 'will' makes the statement neutral.

- A third way of referring to future activity is by using the present progressive forms of verbs. Compare the sentences below.

Mehmood *is going to take* the civil services examination after college.
Mehmood *is taking* the civil services examination next month.

The two sentences have almost the same meaning. Both sentences suggest intention, or planning, on the part of the doer, Mehmood, but the use of the present progressive ('is taking') in the second sentence suggests that the planning is at a more advanced stage and that preparations for the event have already begun. The future event, thus, seems to be more certain.

- Finally, we can refer to future time by using the simple present tense form of the verb. For example:

  The UN secretary general, Kofi Annan, *visits* India and Pakistan next month.

  The use of the simple present suggests that the action or event which is going to take place in the future is part of a programme which has already been finalised and is unlikely to be changed.

  Compare the sentences below to be clear on the four ways of referring to future time.

  Hema Malini *will perform* at the Guruvayoor dance festival next week.

  Hema Malini *is going to perform* at the Guruvayoor dance festival next week.

  Hema Malini *is performing* at the Guruvayoor dance festival next week.

  Hema Malini *performs* at the Guruvayoor dance festival next week.

The use of 'will' in the first sentence makes it a simple announcement of a future event. The use of 'going to' in the second sentence tells us that Hema Malini has plans to perform at the dance festival. The use of 'is performing' in the third sentence tells us that the programme has been arranged and there is a high probability of Hema Malini's performing. (The form 'is performing' shows greater probability than 'going to perform'.) The use of 'performs' in the fourth sentence tells us that the programme has been finalised and that it is certain that Hema Malini will perform.

Exercise 17

Fill in the blanks in the sentences below using 'will' /'shall' + stem, 'going to' + stem, the present continuous or the simple present tense forms of the verbs given in brackets.

a. According to the weather forecast, there .... (be) heavy rainfall all over the state tomorrow.

b. I have decided to become a sculptor when I grow up. I .... (join) an art school.

c. The directors of the company .... (meet) next week. All the arrangements for the meeting are complete.

d. He .... (buy) a new car tomorrow. It is a silver grey Alto.

e. My daughter .... (return) home soon, but she has not made a booking so far.

f. The doctor is busy now but he .... (see) you after an hour.

g. You are neglecting your health. You .... (fall sick).

h. A: What is the programme for the prime minister's visit tomorrow?

   B: Well, the prime minister .... (arrive) at 7.30 a.m. sharp. He .... (go) first to the Raj Bhavan. Then he .... (visit) the State Museum and .... (unveil) a statue of the former chief minister. He .... (return) to Delhi at 8.30 p.m.

i. We .... (visit) Mumbai next Tuesday. We have already bought our tickets.

j. Let us hope they .... (learn) English.

Future progressive

You learnt earlier that the present progressive forms of verbs are used to show action in progress at the present time. For example:

Ramesh *is reading* a book (now).

Similarly, we use the past progressive forms of verbs to show action in progress in the past. For example:

Ramesh *was reading* a book when the train arrived.

In the same way, we can show action in progress in the future by using the progressive (*-ing*) forms of verbs together with 'will + be'. For example:

At 6.00 p.m. tomorrow, I *will be speaking* to some students.

When the boys meet after ten years, all of them *will be working*.

Raji *will be running* the family business by the time her brother leaves college.

Exercise 18

Fill in the blanks in the sentences below, using the future progressive forms of the verbs in brackets.

a. Don't phone me tomorrow morning because I .... (write) some important letters.

b. My friend promised to drop in next week but I don't think he will be able to come as he .... (travel).

c. Raghavan .... (wait) at the airport when you reach Kozhikode tomorrow.

d. Next Monday, at this time, I .... (shake) hands with President Abdul Kalam.

Future Perfect

You have seen how the present perfect tense is used to show that an action is 'complete' at the present time. For example:

He *has finished* his homework.

Again, the use of the past perfect tense shows that an action was completed at some time in the past. For example:

He *had finished* his homework when the teacher asked him for it.

Now look at the following sentence.

Our train reaches Chennai at 9.30 a.m. tomorrow. All the offices *will have opened* by then.

The sentence tells us about two events—(a) the train reaching Chennai and (b) the offices opening—both of which are expected to happen in the future. The use of the future perfect tense 'will have opened' indicates that event (b) will happen at an earlier time in the future than event (a).

Look at some more examples of the use of the future perfect.

The zoo *will have closed* by the time we get there.

Iqbal *will have slept* when you call him.

Before Clara tells Ben about her promotion, he *will have heard* the news.

Thus, the use of 'will'/'shall', together with the perfect form ('have' + participle) tells us that a certain action will be complete by some time in the future.

Exercise 19

Fill in the blanks in the sentences below using the future perfect forms of the verbs in brackets.

a. Rita has decided to deposit Rs 100 into her savings account every month. By the end of the year she .... (save) Rs 1200.

b. Virender Sehwag has played 96 test matches so far. By the end of this tour he .... (play) his hundredth test match.

c. Our examination has begun, and by next Saturday I .... (write) my last paper.

d. Call me two days from now. By then, we .... (takc) a dccision about your transfer.

e. Navnita .... (arrive) by the time you reach home.

Future perfect progressive

The future perfect progressive form of the verb is used to express a special situation and, therefore, we do not commonly use it in speech or writing. Look at the sentence below.

By 2008, Bala *will have been running* the school for ten years.

When I see you next, you *will have been working* at S. M. Pharma for ten months.

In the sentences above, the verb appears in the future perfect progressive tense 'will+have+been+participle'. This form is used when the action indicated by the verb is considered from a point of time in the future, and it is seen as having begun at some earlier point and as continuing up to the future time referred to.

Exercise 20

Fill in the blanks in the sentences below using the future perfect progressive form of the verb in brackets.

a. At this time tomorrow, the man .... (sleep) for twelve hours.

b. When you reach college in the afternoon, the other students .... (attend) classes continuously since morning.

c. They .... (clean) the house since morning when you reach there.

d. Asif .... (teach) for six years at the computer institute by the time his father retires in 2009.

e. When you see me on stage tomorrow, I .... (dance) continuously for four hours.

Exercise 21

Rewrite the following sentences in the tense suggested in brackets.

a. Rosamma is keying in her paper for the conference. (Change into the present perfect tense.)

b. They were working all day. (Change into the simple present tense.)

c. I lived in Kolkata for ten years. (Change into the present perfect progressive tense.)

d. Farukh will buy us chocolates when we visit him. (Change into the future perfect tense.)

e. Huge boulders had rolled down the mountainside when we got there. (Change into the simple past tense.)

f. I am playing a game of cards with my uncle. (Change into the past progressive tense.)

g. Jessie met you at the clinic. (Change into the simple future tense.)

h. The bees have left the hive. (Change into the present progressive tense.)

i. Kunju broke his leg when the vacation started. (Change into the past perfect tense.)

j. Sarabjit Singh has been practising for the tournament since October. (Change into the past perfect progressive tense.)

Subject–Verb Agreement (Concord)

In English, the verb must agree with the subject in number and person. This means that the form of the verb depends, in the case of at least some tenses, on whether its subject is in first, second or third person and on whether it is singular or plural. Let us see how this happens. Study the examples below to understand the pattern. Later, practise using the right verb form with subjects in the first, second and third persons by forming similar sets of sentences using other verbs of your own choice.

1st person	sing.	*I am* a student.
	pl.	We *are* students.
2nd person	sing.	You *are* a student.
	pl.	You *are* students.
3rd person	sing.	He/she *is* a student.
	pl.	They *are* students.

In the sentences above, all of which are in *simple present tense,* thc verb 'be' appears in *three* different forms—'am', 'is' and 'are'—depending on the number and person of the subject. However, the verb 'be' appears in just *two* forms 'was' and 'were' when the sentence is in *simple past tense.*

1st person	sing.	I *was* a student.
	pl.	We *were* students.
2nd person	sing.	You *were* a student.
	pl.	You *were* students.
3rd person	sing.	He/she *was* a student.
	pl.	They *were* students.

The three forms of 'be' in the present tense and its two variants in the past tense is true of the verb whether it appears in a sentence as a main verb or as an auxiliary. The sentences below, where 'be' appears as an auxiliary verb, will make this clear.

I *am working* in Goa./I *was working* in Goa.
We *are working* in Goa./We *were working* in Goa.
Roy, you *are working* in Goa./Roy, you *were working* in Goa.
You *are* both *working* in Goa./You *were* both *working* in Goa.
Appu *is working* in Goa./Appu *was working* in Goa.
They *are working* in Goa./They *were working* in Goa.

In the case of all other verbs (including 'have' and 'do' which like the verb 'be' can be used as main verbs as well as auxiliaries), there are only *two* variant forms, known as 'singular' and 'plural', that are used in agreement with the number and person of the subject when the sentence is in *simple present tense*. The singular form of the verb is used with a subject in third person singular (he/she) and the plural form with all other kinds of subjects. Look at the examples below.

I *have* a new cycle.
We *have* new cycles.
You (sing.) *have* a new cycle.
You (pl.) *have* new cycles.
Sabina *has* a new cycle.
Sabina and Raveena *have* new cycles.

I *do* all the work here.
We *do* all the work here.
You (sing.) *do* all the work here.
You (pl.) *do* all the work here.
Kevin *does* all the work here.
They *do* all the work here.

I *walk* to school everyday.
Vilas and I *walk* to school everyday.
You (sing.) *walk* to school everyday.
You (pl.) *walk* to school everyday.
Jayaraman *walks* to school everyday.
My sisters *walk* to school everyday.

In the last set of sentences above, the verb in the stem + *s* form, 'walks' is said to be the singular form of the verb, and the verb in the stem form, 'walk' is called the plural form of the verb. The choice of the verb form depends as said earlier on the number and person of the subject of a sentence in present tense. Look at some more examples of the use of the singular and plural forms of verbs when the sentences are in simple present tense.

Mr Menon *teaches* English.
The students *study* history in Malayalam.

My sister *writes* poetry.
The boys *play* football.

The boat *leaves* for the bird sanctuary at 6 a.m.
Trains *arrive* on time here.

Note that the agreement rule is not followed if the verb is in the simple past tense. In other words, the form of the verb remains the same irrespective of the number and person of the subject. The only exception to this is, as stated above, the verb 'be', which appears as 'was' or 'were' in the simple past, in its usage as both a main verb and an auxiliary. Look at the sentences below to understand this fully.

I *gave* her fruits.
We *gave* her fruits.

You (sing.) *gave* her fruits.
You (pl.) *gave* her fruits.

The girl *gave* her fruits.
The girls *gave* her fruits.

but
I *was* good at languages.
We *were* cooking dinner.
You (sing.) *were* tired last night.
You (pl.) *were* walking up the hill.
Husain *was* a friendly man.
Husain and Niloufer *were* swimming in the sea.

Exercise 1

Fill in the blanks in the sentences below using the appropriate form (singular or plural) of the verb given in brackets. Use the verbs in the tenses suggested.

a. Bose .... (speak: *simple present*) Kannada fluently.

b. I .... (work: *simple present*) for an NGO in Gwalior.

c. There .... (be: *simple past*) three crows on the tree branch.

d. The boys .... (play: *past progressive*) table tennis.

e. Stephen .... (clear: *present perfect*) the table.

f. The planes .... (approach: *present progressive*) the airport.

g. You .... (stay: *past progressive*) alone in that huge house.

h. Natasha and her sister .... (go: *simple past*) for a walk in the park.

i. They .... (paint: *simple present*) very well.

j. Reena .... (want: *simple present*) to go to Chennai for her holiday, but her friends .... (prefer: *simple present*) to go to Mumbai.

k. Ahmed and Rafi .... (be: *simple past*) on their way to school. They .... (run: *past progressive*) to catch the bus as they .... (be: *simple past*) late.

l. Mr Kutty .... (move: *present progressive*) into his new house next week. He .... (invite: *present perfect*) all his friends to a house-warming party and we .... (accept: *present perfect*) his invitation.

Although the agreement rule is applicable in most cases, it has to be used with care in some special cases, which we shall look at now.

- When the subject consists of two singular or plural nouns (or pronouns) joined by 'and', the plural form of the verb is normally used. For example:

The president and the vice president *are coming* to the meeting.

In the above sentence, the two nouns joined by 'and' refer to two different people. But in case the two nouns refer to the same person, the singular form of the verb is used. For example:

The president and chief executive of the company *has arrived.*

Here the two nouns ('president' and 'chief executive') refer to the same person.

- If the two nouns joined together by 'and' are thought of as a single 'thing', the singular form of the verb is used. For example:

  Idli and sambar *is* my favourite breakfast.

- When we refer to an amount or quantity of something (distance, money, etc.), it is used with the singular form of the verb. For example:

  150 kilometres *is* not a great distance.
  Ten thousand rupees *is* a fair price for this car.

- The singular form of the verb is used if the subject consists of two singular nouns joined together by 'either. . . or' and 'neither . . . nor', as in the following examples.

  Either the president or the secretary *has signed* this document.
  Neither Robert nor Abdul *has come* to the meeting.

  However, if the nouns connected by 'either . . . or'/'neither . . . nor' are plural, the plural form of the verb is used. For example:

  Either my children or their friends *have written* this letter.
  Neither the girls nor the boys *have* any knowledge of this matter.

- When pronouns such as 'everyone, 'someone', 'no one', etc. are used as the subject, the singular form of the verb is used. For example:

  Everyone *wants* to succeed.

No one *knows* the answer.

Pronouns such as 'everyone', 'everybody' 'no one,' 'nobody', 'someone', 'somebody', etc., are considered to be singular and therefore take the singular form of the verb. However, note that they are followed by plural pronouns such as 'they', 'them', 'their', etc. For example:

Everyone *has finished* their work.
Nobody *is allowed* to go unless they have finished their work.

The plural pronouns 'their' and 'them' are used in these sentences because pronouns like 'everyone' and 'nobody' can be used to refer to both men and women. We use the plural pronoun to avoid saying something like the following which sounds awkward.

Everyone *has finished* his or her homework.

- Some nouns ending in '*-s*' are considered plural in form and take plural verbs. These nouns do not have singular forms. For example:

  Her clothes *are* very expensive.
  His trousers *have become* too tight.
  Where *are* your spectacles (glasses)?

  Some other nouns of this kind are: 'arms' (meaning 'weapons'), 'belongings', 'congratulations,' 'goods,' 'surroundings,' 'thanks' and 'troops'.

- Uncountable nouns, such as 'baggage', 'equipment', 'furniture' and 'luggage' are treated as singular nouns. Hence, they take singular verbs only. For example:

  Your baggage *is* heavy.
  The equipment *is* expensive.

- Collective nouns, such as, 'government,' 'public,' 'team,' 'party' and 'media,' can take either a singular or a plural verb. For example:

  The committee *is* investigating this matter.
  The committee *are* of the view that the investigation should be completed quickly.

In the first sentence we think of a 'committee' as an undivided group, but in the second we are referring to the individuals who form the committee.

Exercise 2

Fill in the blanks in the sentences below using the appropriate form (singular or plural) of the verb given in brackets. Use the verbs in the tenses suggested.

a. The young children in this school .... (have: simple present) yoga classes twice a week.

b. Both the rice and the curd .... (be: simple past) fresh and tasty.

c. The rice and curd which the restaurant serves .... (be: simple present) fresh and tasty.

d. Rs 10,000 a month .... (be: simple present) a good salary for a beginner.

e. Neither Murali nor Tara .... (know: simple present) the answer to this question.

f. Either the boys or their parents .... (collect: present perfect) the report cards.

g. The furniture in these rooms .... (be: simple present) very expensive.

h. Each chapter in these books .... (need: simple present) to be read carefully.

i. Everyone .... (look at: present progressive) the beautiful paintings on the walls.

j. The information you gave me (happen: simple present) to be incorrect.

k. The jury .... (look: past progressive) at one another with puzzled expressions on their faces.

l. The luggage .... (fall: present progressive) off the rack.

m. Physics .... (be: simple present) my favourite subject.

n. Either you or your sisters ...... (use: present perfect) these brushes.

o. The public .... (has: simple present) a right to know the facts of the case.

The Passive Voice

Look at the sentences below.

John *repaired* the toaster.
subj. verb obj.

The toaster *was repaired* by John.
subj. verb obj.

In the first sentence, the subject of the verb is 'John', who is the performer of the action, and its object is 'the toaster', which is affected by the action. The verb 'repaired', in other words, expresses the action done by the subject of the sentence, John. In such a case, when the subject of a sentence is also the performer of the action indicated by the verb, it is said to be in active voice. In contrast, the subject of the second sentence is 'the toaster', towards which the action of the performer is directed, and which is affected by it. Here the verb 'was repaired' is said to be in passive voice and the preposition 'by' links it to the following object noun, 'John'. In other words, while the subject of a verb in the active voice is the 'doer' or 'agent' of the action expressed by it, the subject of a verb in the passive voice is the 'receiver' of the action indicated by the verb. Some more examples of sentences in active and passive voice are given below.

Leena dropped the spoons into the sink.
The spoons were dropped into the sink by Leena.
The church choir will present some well-known hymns.
Some well-known hymns will be presented by the church choir.
The retired defence officers in the town are organising a show.
A show is being organised by the retired defence officers in the town.

When the verb in the active voice takes two objects, it is more usual to make the indirect or personal object the subject of the verb in the passive voice. In the sentences below, the indirect object appears as the subject of the verb in the passive voice.

Vidya gave Maria a present.
(subj. + verb + indir. obj. + dir. obj.)
Maria was given a present by Vidya.

Shaila will send me the journal.
I will be sent the journal by Shaila.

The teacher is showing the students sample test papers.
The students are being shown sample test papers by the teacher.

However, the direct object of the verb does appear as the subject of a sentence in passive voice when there is a need to highlight it for some reason. This happens in the following sentence in passive voice.

The social welfare organisation gave the tsunami victims food and medicines.
Food and medicines were given to the tsunami victims by the social welfare organisation.

When the object of a verb in active voice is not a pronoun, noun or noun phrase, but a clause introduced by 'that', the corresponding sentence in passive begins with 'it'. Look at the following sentences.

Everyone says that this government should go.
It is said that this government should go. (Reference to the doer—'by everyone'—is felt to be unnecessary and is usually omitted.)

They believed that the child was safe.
It was believed that the child was safe. ('by them' usually omitted)

We know that many species of plants and animals are in danger of extinction.
It is known that many species of plants and animals are in danger of extinction. ('by us' omitted)

Note that in all the sentences given above, the doer(s) of the action appearing as subjects of the sentences in active voice, do not refer to a particular person or persons and are therefore omitted when the sentence is changed into passive voice. However, in other sentences of the above kind, the doer of the action appears with the verb in passive voice if it happens to refer to a particular person or persons. The following sentences will illustrate this point.

Vinu feels that the weather will improve.
It is felt by Vinu that the weather will improve.

Parents hope that their children will grow up to be fine human beings.
It is hoped by parents that their children will grow up to be fine human beings.

The scientists argued that a fair amount of original research was being done in the country.
It was argued by the scientists that a fair amount of original research was being done in the country.

Since the noun in the object position in an active sentence moves to the subject position when the sentence is changed into passive, it is easy to understand that intransitive verbs, which do not take an object, appear only in active forms.

The baby *slept*.
Gopi *ran* fast.
I *sat down*.

Although the active and passive forms of verbs have almost the same meaning, the active is usually the more natural way of expressing an idea. Thus, the sentence 'Suresh drinks coffee at breakfast', in active voice, is more natural and hence more commonly used in both speech and writing than the passive 'Coffee is drunk at breakfast by Suresh.' Further, the passive voice is not just an alternative form, but it has its own uses. There is a clear difference in emphasis in sentences of the two types.

The passive voice is used specifically in the following situations.

- when we want to draw attention to the receiver, rather than the performer, of the action

The soldiers were given a warm reception by the people.

- when the doer of the action is not really relevant to the context, is unknown, or is too well understood to require mention

  The house was cleaned before the guests arrived.
  The windowpanes were broken.
  The rioters were arrested.

- in newspaper reports and scientific and technical writing where the focus is on the event or process described rather than on the agent

  People in the earthquake affected areas were evacuated and sent to relief camps.
  The mixture of hydrochloric acid and salt was shaken vigorously.

- when we wish to make a statement sound impersonal or less unpleasant

  The work has to be completed by Friday.

- when talking about natural calamities like earthquakes and typhoons

  The fishing village was completely destroyed by the tsunami.

- when we wish to conceal the identity of the performer of an action

  It is confirmed that the leaders of the two countries will hold high-level talks soon.

- when people in general are the performers of actions

  Today, a lot of money is being spent on food, clothes and entertainment.

The form of the verb in the passive voice depends on its tense. The table below will show you how this happens and will help you learn how to use the passive voice.

tense	**active form**	**passive form**
present simple	*eat, eats* (They eat salads.)	*am/ is/are + eaten* (Salads are eaten by them.)
present continuous	*am/is/are + eating*	*am/is/are + being eaten*

	(They are eating salads.)	(Salads are being eaten by them.)
present perfect	*has/have + eaten*	*has/have +been eaten*
	(They have eaten salads.)	(Salads have been eaten by them.)
past simple	*ate*	*was/were + eaten*
	(They ate salads.)	(Salads were eaten by them.)
past continuous	*was/were eating*	*was/were + being eaten*
	(They were eating salads.)	(Salads were being eaten by them.)
past perfect	*had eaten*	*had + been eaten*
	(They had eaten salads.)	(Salads had been eaten by them.)
future	*will/shall eat*	*will/shall be eaten*
	(They will eat salads.)	(Salads will be eaten by them.)
future perfect	*will/shall + have eaten*	*will/shall + have been eaten*
	(They will have eaten salads.)	(Salads will have been eaten by them.)

Exercise 1

Rewrite the following sentences in the passive voice, using the 'by + object' phrase only if you think it is really necessary.

a. The judge acquitted the man of the crime.

b. Nina is making a bouquet of roses and lilies.

c. People believe all that appear in newspapers.

d. The crows built a nest on the jackfruit tree.

e. My sister will cook dinner tonight.

f. The teacher had prepared the students well for the test they took.

g. The man outside the store was ringing a bell.
h. Maya has left all the windows open.
i. They were carrying baskets of flowers and sweets.
j. You will have read the book by the time I return.

Now look at the following commands and see how they can be changed into passive voice. Note the italicised words to understand how this is done.

Give him some money. (active voice)
Let him *be given* some money. (passive voice)

Make the bed. (active voice)
Let the bed *be made*. (passive voice)

Give everyone food and water. (active voice)
Let everyone *be given* food and water. (passive voice)

Look at what happens when questions are changed into passive voice.

Did you understand the lesson?
Was the lesson understood by you?

Do they sell building material?
Is building material sold by them?

Will Neha buy the two-wheeler?
Will the two-wheeler be bought by Neha?

Can we change the curtains?
Can the curtains be changed?

Should Vikram have an injection?
Should an injection be had by Vikram?

Where does Soman keep the car keys?
Where are the car keys kept by Soman?

When did Padma shut down the computer?
When was the computer shut down by Padma?

Note that the active voice is the usual, preferred form in the case of the two types of sentences above.

Exercise 2

Rewrite the following sentences in the passive voice, using the 'by + object' phrase only if you think it is really necessary.

a. Find the lost documents.
b. When did you read the story?
c. Can you pay the tuition fees tomorrow?
d. Build a bridge across the river.
e. Does Lata read science fiction?
f. Carry the injured to the ambulance.
g. Will the rising water flood the fields?
h. When do they open the gate?
i. Send presents to the bride.
j. Is the nurse dressing the wound?

Exercise 3

Do as directed in the brackets at the end of each sentence below.

a. The doctor will ask us many questions. (Change into passive voice.)
b. It was noticed that the attendance in the school was picking up. (Change into active voice.)
c. We can repair this toaster easily. (Change into passive voice.)
d. A book on naturopathy is being published by the Ayurveda College. (Change into active voice.)
e. The people in the auditorium saw a man running up to the stage. (Change into passive voice.)
f. The dogs have not been fed today. (Change into active voice.)
g. Everybody praises Timothy's illustrations. (Change into passive voice.)
h. The antique was stolen. (Change into active voice.)
i. Can Bipin set up a meeting for us with the director? (Change into passive voice.)
j. Women are still denied the right to vote in some parts of the world. (Change into active voice.)

Direct and Indirect Speech

There are two ways of reporting the words spoken by other people. The first way is to repeat the exact words of the speaker and enclose them within quotation marks, and this way of reporting is called *direct speech*. (Either single or double quotation marks may be used to enclose the words being reported—the choice is really a matter of style.)

> Tara said, 'It is time to leave for the meeting.'
> 'Come home early,' said Mr Shamim to his son.
> The lawyer said to her client, 'Do you have the registration papers?'
> The woman said to Swati, 'Where do you stay?'
> 'What a beautiful bracelet!' Jacob said.

Now look at the following sentences, where you report the words of the speaker in your own words, making some changes in grammatical construction. This form of reporting is known as *indirect* or *reported* speech, which we usually use in reporting what others said.

> Tara *said that* it was time to leave for the meeting.
> Mr Shamim *ordered* his son *to* come home early.
> The lawyer *asked* her client *if* he had the registration papers.
> The woman *asked* Swati where she stayed.
> Jacob *exclaimed that* it was a beautiful bracelet.

The verbs 'said', 'asked' and 'exclaimed', used to report the words of the speaker, are referred to as the *reporting verbs*. The reporting verb used depends on the type of sentence reported. Thus, while 'said' or 'told' are used to report statements, 'asked' is preferred when the reported sentence happens to be a question, 'requested' or 'ordered' or 'told' when it is a command, and 'exclaimed' in the case of exclamatory sentences. Besides these reporting verbs that are commonly used, the verbs given below are also used to report the four types of sentences.

- *statements (affirmative and negative):* affirm, state, declare, assert, propose, allege, maintain, assure, announce, protest, swear, agree, promise, remark, remind, explain, etc.

- *questions:* enquire (of someone), question, query, wonder, etc.
- *commands and requests:* command, direct, forbid, warn, ask, beg, plead, pray, advise, etc.
- *exclamations:* cry, scream, etc.

Go back to the sentences given above to note the words used to connect the reporting verbs in different types of sentences with the speech being reported. Thus, the connective 'that' is used in reporting statements and exclamatory sentences, while 'if/whether' is used in the case of yes–no questions. However, note that in the case of Q-word questions (beginning with 'what', 'where', when', which', why' 'who' and 'how'), instead of the connectives 'if' and 'whether', the Q-word in the sentence is followed by the subject and verb. When a request or command in direct speech is changed into indirect speech, the infinitive form of the verb is used, such as, 'to come' in the example given above.

Now let us look at some more sentences to understand the changes that happen to the verb in the sentence within inverted commas when changed into indirect speech. First, note that the form of the verb in the reported sentence does not change if the reporting verb is in present simple, present perfect or future tense.

> Damu *says,* 'Priya *is working* in Ahmedabad.' (direct speech)
> Damu *says* that Priya *is working* in Ahmedabad. (indirect speech)
>
> Many people *have said,* 'Shirin *treated* us well.' (direct speech)
> Many people *have said* that Shirin *treated* them well. (indirect speech)
>
> You *will say*, 'The tea *is* too sweet.' (direct speech)
> You *will say* that the tea *is* too sweet. (indirect speech)

However, the form of the verb within inverted commas changes to the corresponding past tense when the reporting verb is in past simple tense. Look at the following pairs of sentences, all of which have the reporting verb in past simple tense, and note how the verb in the reported sentence changes.

- When the verb in the sentence in direct speech is in present simple tense, it changes to the past simple tense.

  Gopu *said*, 'The bell *rings* at 9 a.m.' (direct speech)
  Gopu *said* that the bell *rang* at 9 a.m. (indirect speech)

- When the verb in the sentence in direct speech is in present continuous tense, it changes to the past continuous tense.

  Gopu *said*, 'The bell *is ringing*.' (direct speech)
  Gopu *said* that the bell *was ringing*. (indirect speech)

- When the verb in the sentence in direct speech is in present perfect tense, it changes to the past perfect tense.

  Gopu *said*, 'The bell *has rung*.' (direct speech)
  Gopu *said* that the bell *had rung*. (indirect speech)

- When the verb in the sentence in direct speech is in present perfect continuous tense, it changes to the past perfect continuous tense.

  Gopu *said*, 'The bell *has been ringing*.' (direct speech)
  Gopu *said* that the bell *had been ringing*. (indirect speech)

- When the verb in the sentence in direct speech is also in past simple tense, it changes to the past perfect tense.

  Gopu *said*, 'The bell *rang*.' (direct speech)
  Gopu *said* that the bell *had rung*. (indirect speech)

- When the verb in the sentence in direct speech is in past continuous tense, it changes to the past perfect continuous tense.

  Gopu *said*, 'The bell *was ringing*.' (direct speech)
  Gopu *said* that the bell *had been ringing*. (indirect speech)

- When the verb in the sentence in direct speech comes with the auxiliary verb 'will' (or 'shall') to indicate future action, the auxiliary changes to its past tense form 'would'.

  Gopu *said*, 'The bell *will ring*.' (direct speech)
  Gopu said that the bell would ring. (indirect speech)

- Similarly, modal auxiliaries 'can' and 'may' change to their corresponding past tense forms 'could' and 'might' in indirect speech.

Gopu *said*, 'Alex *can ring* the bell.' (direct speech)
Gopu *said* that Alex *could ring* the bell. (indirect speech)

Gopu *said*, 'Alex *may ring* the bell.' (direct speech)
Gopu *said* that Alex *might ring* the bell. (indirect speech)

- Modal auxiliaries 'must' and 'should' either remain unchanged or change to 'had to' or 'would have to'. The modal auxiliary 'ought to' remains unchanged.

Gopu *said*, 'Alex *must ring* the bell.' (direct speech)
Gopu *said* that Alex *had to ring* the bell. (indirect speech)

Gopu *said*, 'Alex *ought to ring the bell.*' (direct speech)
Gopu *said* that Alex *ought to ring* the bell. (indirect speech)

There are, however, situations when the simple past form of the verb in direct speech remains unchanged in indirect speech even when the reporting verb is in past tense. Look at the following pairs of sentences.

The speaker *said*, 'The United Nations *adopted* the Human Rights Charter in 1948.'
The speaker *said* that the United Nations *adopted* the Human Rights Charter in 1948.

They *said*, 'If it *rained* for three months in the desert, farming would be possible there.'
They *said* that if it *rained* for three months in the desert, farming would be possible there.

Mira *said*, 'When the boy *picked up* the baby, his sister *smiled.*'
Mira *said* that when the boy *picked up* the baby, his sister *smiled.*

In the first pair of sentences, the speaker refers to a historical event, in the second pair of sentences the speaker refers to a hypothetical or imagined condition and in the third pair of sentences, the speaker describes two events/actions occurring at about the same time.

Similarly, the present simple form of the verb does not change into past tense if the reported sentence expresses (a) a habitual action/something that happens to be true at the time of reporting, (b) a universal truth/scientific fact or (c) something that is expected to happen in the future (at the time of reporting). The sentences below will illustrate this.

> She *said*, 'Nitin *takes* the 8 o'clock train every day.'
> She *said* that Nitin *takes* the 8 o'clock train every day.

> I *said*, 'Water *is* essential for life.'
> I *said* that water *is* essential for life.

> Tina *said* two minutes ago, 'The theatre group *is visiting* Thrissur soon.'
> Tina *said* two minutes ago that the theatre group *is visiting* Thrissur soon.

When sentences are changed from direct to indirect speech, personal and possessive pronouns also change their form. The changes depend on who the speaker, the person spoken to and the person reporting the speech are. Look at the following sentences that illustrate the changes pronouns undergo when sentences in direct speech are changed into indirect speech. All changes in pronouns have been italicised so that you may spot them easily.

> I said to her, 'Will *you* teach mc knitting?'
> I asked her whether *she* would teach me knitting.

> He said to us, '*You* can borrow *my* pen.'
> He told us that *we* could borrow *his* pen.

> They said to me, 'Oh, we are delighted to be in *your* class!'
> They exclaimed that they were delighted to be in *my* class.

> You said, 'Raj, stop taking *my* things without asking *me*.'
> You ordered Raj to stop taking *your* things without asking *you*.

> She said, '*My* brother has gone out.'
> She said that *her* brother had gone out.

> You said to me, '*You* must give *me your* email id.'
> You told me that *I* must give *you my* email id.

The last set of changes that occur when sentences in direct speech are reported in indirect speech is seen in the form of demonstratives (this, these) and adverbs of time and place (now, ago, today, yesterday, here, etc). These changes are shown in the table below for your easy reference.

direct speech	**indirect speech**
now	then
here	there
ago	before, earlier
today/tonight	that day/that night
tomorrow	the next day/the following day
yesterday	the previous day/ the day before
last month	the previous month
next Thursday	the following Thursday
this/these	that/those

Look at some sentences for examples of changes involving the above words and phrases.

Sudha said to us, 'Let us go to the UP state emporium *today*.'
Sudha suggested that we go to the UP state emporium *that day*.

His classmate said to Akash, 'Will you receive my grandmother at the station next *week?*'
His classmate asked Akash whether he would receive her (or his) grandmother at the station the *following week*.

The man said to me, 'Don't put your things *here*.'
The man ordered me not to put my things *there*.

You said, 'Sonali gave me *this* handbag.'
You said that Sonali gave you *that* handbag.

Udit said to his wife, 'When are you going out *tomorrow*.'
Udit asked his wife when she was going out the *next day*.

Shanti said, 'I live in Shillong *now*.'
Shanti said that she lived in Shillong *then*.

We said, 'Thank you for helping us *yesterday*.'
We thanked him/her/them for helping us the *previous day*.

Sometimes what you wish to report consists of more than one sentence. In such cases, the sentences could either be of the same type or else they could be of different types, say, a statement and a question. Remember that you will follow the patterns explained above to change each of the separate sentences into indirect speech, and combine them if you wish into one sentence using appropriate connectives, such as, 'and' and 'but'. Look at the examples below.

> Kamala said to her husband, 'I cannot find the garden hose. Did you take it?' (direct speech)
> Kamala *told* her husband that she could not find the garden hose *and asked* him if he had taken it. (indirect speech)

> The fisherman said to his companions, 'What a terrible storm! Let us, however, wait for a while before returning to the shore.'
> The fisherman *cried* that it was a terrible storm *but suggested* to his companions that they wait for a while before returning to the shore.

Exercise 1

Rewrite the following sentences in indirect speech. Try to use reporting verbs such as 'assure' and 'promise', which indicate the function performed by the reported sentence(s).

a. Hasan said, 'I am returning to Nagpur next Saturday.'
b. 'If I see Jai, I shall certainly bring him here,' said Dr Singh.
c. 'The birds are flying away,' Kavita says.
d. 'Helen writes very well,' said her friend.
e. I said to the men, 'You can keep your boxes in the room.'
f. 'Kurien built a house in my village last year,' said Chinnu.
g. Everybody will say to them, 'You did a great job.'
h. The officer said, 'Some of the animals have been saved.'
i. The teacher said, 'Hitler became the chancellor of Germany in 1933.'
j. 'Sania has been looking after my child since yesterday,' said the woman.
k. 'Let us have a farewell dinner for our chairperson,' the director said.

l. Sunita said to me, 'Your letter will not reach me as I am leaving the city today.'

Exercise 2

Rewrite the following sentences in indirect speech.

a. The nurse said to the patient, 'Has the pain become worse?'
b. 'Did you know that I am your cousin's colleague?' said Kala to me.
c. He said to you, 'What is the price of this tray?'
d. 'Are you walking with me to the beach?' the boy said to his friends.
e. 'Where was Alka when the telephone rang?' they said to him.
f. Anju said to Neil, 'Which shirt did you send to the laundry?'
g. Everybody will say to her, 'How does it feel to be home?'
h. 'Do you practise regularly?' said the coach to the athlete.
i. The guest said, 'Why is the room so stuffy?'
j. 'When can you meet me?' Prem said to his daughter.

Exercise 3

Rewrite the following sentences in indirect speech.

a. Tony said to his teacher, 'Please give me another day to complete my work.'
b. 'Take the certificates that you left here two days ago,' said the principal to the student.
c. 'Don't eat fruits and vegetables without first washing them,' said Lola to us.
d. The general said to the soldiers, 'Take up positions to defend our camp against the enemy.'
e. 'Let the old people, the women and the children be allowed to go unharmed,' said the pilot.
f. 'How fortunate it is that you are here!' said Basant to his brother.
g. The managing director said, 'Mr Gupta, will you be going to Sri Lanka next month? There is an international conference on herbal medicine in Colombo on the 15th.'

h. 'What a pleasant surprise! I was longing to see you,' said Shruti to her mother.

i. Uncle said, 'Sharan, let us leave the car at the service station. Uma will pick it up tomorrow evening.'

j. Minu said to them, 'Please sit down. Did you want to speak to me about something?'

Exercise 4

Rewrite the following sentences in direct speech.

a. Tania requested her friend to lend her an umbrella.

b. They told me that I could take the boat that was going to the Andaman islands.

c. Padma congratulated Franson on his promotion.

d. The officer asked the passenger if she had anything to declare.

e. Shah said that his mother would leave the next day.

f. We promised Rashmi that we would meet her there.

g. He asked me whether I played cards.

h. Niti apologised to Shobha for losing her bracelet.

i. The girl told her brother that they were late for the meeting.

j. Aman told the salesperson that he was looking for Dan Brown's latest novel.

Negative Sentences

Statements made by a speaker can be affirmative if they declare *what happened*, *what was said or done*, etc. They can, on the other hand, be negative if they state *what did not happen*, *what was not said or done*, etc. Look at the sentences given below.

> The show *will start* in an hour.
> Kunal *was smiling* at me.
>
> The cows *have returned* to the shed.
> A flyover *is being constructed* at Patel Chowk.

All the sentences above make affirmative, or positive statements about a person, object or event. Now look at the following negative sentences corresponding to the these affirmative statements.

The show *will not start* in an hour.
Kunal *was not smiling* at me.
The cows *have not returned* to the shed.
A flyover *is not being constructed* at Patel Chowk.

Note that affirmative sentences are changed into negative ones by adding 'not' between the auxiliary verb and the main verb. For example, in the sentence 'The show will *not* start in an hour', 'not' is inserted between 'will', which is an auxiliary verb, and 'start', a main verb.

In the case of an affirmative sentence that has only a main verb, the auxiliary verb 'do' is used (in its appropriate tense form and in agreement with the person and number of the subject), and this is followed by 'not' and the stem form of the main verb.

The plane *took off* from this runway. (affirmative)
The plane *did not take off* from this runway. (negative)

Vijaya *drives* well. (affirmative)
Vijaya *does not drive* well. (negative)

They *like* travelling. (affirmative)
They *do not like* travelling. (negative)

In imperative sentences, the negative is formed by putting the words 'do not' at the beginning of the sentence, before the main verb.

Put away the crockery.
Do not put away the crockery.

Give him your book.
Do not give him your book.

Look at this.
Do not look at this.

It is useful to remember that sometimes the contracted form of the negative 'not' is linked to the preceding auxiliary verb. It is also possible to link the contracted form of the auxiliary to the subject noun or pronoun before it. These contracted forms are commonly used in informal and spoken English.

They *aren't* (are not) eating ice-cream.
You *don't* (do not) understand this, do you?
We're (we are) not amused.
Mother's (mother is) not leaving tonight.

Exercise

Change the following affirmative sentences into negative sentences.

a. I am a doctor.
b. She wants to learn ballet.
c. Include this amount in your bill.
d. She returned to India in a month.
e. Basheer is happy with the arrangements.
f. They have a lot of work to complete.
g. Tara was absent today.
h. Please say this to him.
i. The solution was clear.
j. You did Kirti a favour.
k. The boat was rocking violently.
l. Turn the car.
m. Stephen and his friend were picking guavas from the tree.
n. We will buy pearls in Hyderabad.
o. They have been spending a lot on clothes.

Question Tags

Question tags are short questions that are added on to statements for the purpose of asking for the listener's confirmation or agreement. They are usually used in spoken English or in informal writing. A question tag consists of a verb followed by a pronoun corresponding to the subject of the statement. It must be noted that the tense of the verb in the question tag is always the same as that of the verb in the preceding statement. If the predicate of the statement has an auxiliary verb before the main verb (for example, 'is arriving'), then the auxiliary verb appears in the question tag. Look at the sentences below.

Kumar *is* arriving today, isn't he?
The woman *can* play the violin, can't she?
I *am* your friend, aren't I?
You *have* met Ruma, haven't you?
Mallika *was* in the gym, wasn't she?
Sanjay and Paru *will* help us, won't they?
Father and I *were* late, weren't we?
The weather *has* improved, hasn't it?
All of us *should* do our best, shouldn't we?
The Kuriens *are* such wonderful people, aren't they?

However, if the finite verb in the statement consists of only a main verb (for example, 'gave'), the auxiliary 'do' functions as the verb in the tag. Look at the following sentences.

Bharat *gave* you his muffler, didn't he?
The flowers *smell* wonderful, don't they?
We *showed* Kumar the photographs, didn't we?
You *live* in Nasik, don't you?
I *came* home early yesterday, didn't I?
Gauri *does* her best to win every match, doesn't she?
The minister *spoke* well at the conference, didn't he?
The tourists *saw* many elephants at Thekkady, didn't they?
Tina *runs* very fast, doesn't she?
The cutlets Susan made *taste* good, don't they?
Madurai *is* an ancient city, isn't it?

When question tags follow statements with indefinite pronouns like 'everyone' and 'nobody', the pronoun 'they' is used in the tag.

Everybody is asleep, aren't *they*?

Similarly, 'this' and 'that' are replaced in the tag by 'it'.

This is a new shirt, isn't *it*?

In order to use question tags, you need to remember another point with regard to their form. All positive statements are followed by a negative tag, and negative statements take a positive tag. The sentences below should make this clear.

Hamid will lay the table, won't he?
It is not very cold, is it?
Prasad will come back, won't he?
The animals have not been fed, have they?
We work hard, don't we?
They don't work hard, do they?
You should have left by now, shouldn't you?
Neelima has not heard about this, has she?
This cloth feels good, doesn't it?
The book has not been published, has it?

However, when statements are affirmative in form but are negative in meaning because of the presence of words like 'hardly', 'barely' and 'never', they are followed by affirmative tags.

Wilfred *never* takes time off from work, does he?
She can *hardly* walk, can she?
Mani *seldom* writes letters, does she?

Further, note that the question tag can be used with two intonation patterns: (a) a falling one when the speaker is sure he is right, and is only asking for the listener's agreement and (b) a rising tone when the speaker is not really sure about what he said and seeks a yes–no response.

Finally, imperatives can be made to sound more polite by adding question tags to them.

Shut the door, will you?
Make some tea, will you?

Exercise 1

Rewrite the following sentences, adding question tags to them. Remember to place a comma between the tag and the preceding statement.

a. Kranti repaired the clock.
b. It is not dark.
c. They were going to the lake.
d. The bus had left by the time we got there.
e. You are trying to find someone.
f. Pavan has not kept his word.
g. The bread will become soggy.
h. His parents would not have left before yesterday.
i. I can see how earnest you are.
j. Shanta loves icecream.
k. The bus skidded on the wet road.
l. Vimala sells wooden toys.
m. None of the workers left early.
n. You haven't left the door open.
o. The clothes in the store are priced very high.

Exercise 2

Correct the following sentences.

a. They won't leave the baby alone at home, will they not?
b. Cynthia looked pretty in the green dress, isn't it?
c. Gardening used to be Hari's favourite pastime, doesn't it?
d. We will grow tomatoes and carrots, will we?
e. I haven't met the Menons, did I?
f. Mala couldn't run, can she?
g. Mother plans to work late in the office, didn't she?
h. The astronauts are ready to enter the spacecraft, isn't he?
i. There were ten chocolates in the paper bag, weren't they not?
j. The water is getting cold, does it?

Simple, Compound and Complex Sentences

One of the ways of classifying sentences is by identifying them as being simple, compound or complex. This grouping is done on the basis of the number and types of clauses (which are groups of words with a subject and a finite verb) in the sentence.

A simple sentence consists of a subject and a predicate that has only one finite verb. In other words, a simple sentence consists of a single clause. For example, in the sentences below, the italicised words are finite verb forms indicating the simple past, simple present and present progressive tenses.

> Balu *skipped.*
> My sister *writes* poetry.
> Many young girls *are opting* for aerospace engineering.
> The man *entered* a low mud hut.

The above sentences represent basic structures, and it is possible to expand these simple sentences by adding adjectives, adverbs and phrases.

> Balu *skipped* excitedly.
> My talented sister *writes* poetry.
> Inpired by Kalpana Chawla, many young girls *are opting* for aerospace engineering.
> Having crossed the paddy field, the man *entered* a low mud hut.

Note that in the phrases at the beginning of the last two sentences above, 'inspired' and 'having crossed' are not finite verbs, but past participle and perfect participle forms, which do not reflect tense, number or person. Thus, in the following sentences, 'inspired' and 'having crossed' are non-finite verbs, while 'opt', 'opts' and 'opted' as well as 'entered', 'is entering' and 'are entering' are finite verbs.

> Inspired by Kalpana Chawla, many young girls *opt* for aerospace engineering.
> Inspired by Kalpana Chawla, the young girl *opts* for aerospace engineering.
> Inspired by Kalpana Chawla, the young girl *opted* for aerospace engineering.
>
> Having crossed the paddy field, the man *entered* a low mud hut.

> Having crossed the paddy field, the man *is entering* a low mud hut.
> Having crossed the paddy field, the men *are entering* a low mud hut.

Look at some more examples of simple sentences. Each of these sentences has only one finite verb, which has been italicised to set it apart from the non-finite verb forms that occur in some of the sentences. Other than the past participle and perfect participle forms, you will find two other non-finite verbs in the sentences below. These are the present participle (e.g., 'seeing') and the infinitive (e.g., 'to call').

> *Open* the door.
> Lions *roar*.
> Where *is* Praveen?
> The car *sped* along the road.
> Sarah *did* well in the test in spite of being unwell.
> James and Priya *are* good friends.
> Seeing the butterflies, the children *clapped* their hands in joy.
> Having learnt to cook, Abdullah *will invite* everybody to a meal sometime.
> Venu *loved* visiting his grandmother.
> You *play* the tabla very well.
> Her people *elected* her their spokesperson.
> Prakash *ran* to call his father.

A compound sentence has two or more main clauses (which can stand alone as independent sentences) linked by coordinating conjunctions. For example, in the sentences below, the main clauses are joined by the coordinating conjunctions 'or', 'but' and 'yet'.

> You can send the packet by courier *or* Raj can take it with him.
> Sheila asked Anil to stay for lunch, *but* he left.
> It was raining, *yet* we went shopping.

Note that in the above sentences each of the two clauses can be an independent sentence, beginning with a capital letter and ending with a full stop. Further, the subject of the second clause can be omitted or replaced with the corresponding pronoun in case it happens to be the same as that of the first one.

Jyoti went to Chandigarh *and* worked as a librarian.

Kiran and Unni read the book, *but* they did not like it.

Some other coordinating conjunctions used to form compound sentences are: 'either . . . or', 'nor', 'neither . . . nor', 'still', 'for', 'so', 'therefore', 'not only . . . but also', and 'nevertheless'.

Exercise 1

Combine each of the following pairs of simple sentences into a compound sentence, using the coordinating conjunctions given above. You can refer to the given example.

I rang the bell. Nobody came to the door.
I rang the bell, but nobody came to the door.

a. Kripa will stay in a hotel. Kripa will stay with friends in the city.

b. The clothes were put out in the morning. The clothes are not dry.

c. Abu is leaving for Chennai today. Abu's father is leaving for Rourkela tomorrow.

d. The boy can rest at home. The boy can go to school.

e. Arun helped Sally fill in the application form. Arun posted the application form for Sally.

f. The workers did an excellent job. Their employer gave them a huge bonus.

g. My dog has not been active. He has not eaten all day.

h. We were just given an hour to prepare for the test. We did the test well.

i. Puneet is clever. Puneet is kind.

j. The problem is complex. It is interesting.

Exercise 2

Change the following simple sentences into compound sentences. You can refer to the given example.

Despite running all the way, Alka was late for college.

Alka ran all the way, but she was late for college.

a. In spite of being new to the place, Tanu got everybody to support her cause.
b. Having finished work for the day, we left the office.
c. To my surprise, Mini arrived in the morning with a pup in her arms.
d. It was not dark even at seven in the evening.
e. Walking down the road, Sam looked at the lovely houses on both sides.
f. Bored with the hostel food, the students decided to cook a meal for themselves.
g. All the flights have been cancelled owing to the bad weather.
h. Madhu had the options of working or enrolling for an advanced course in computer application.
i. Being exhausted after the climb, we rested on the hilltop for a while.
j. Seema called her uncle to ask him for an address.

A sentence with a main clause and one or more subordinate clauses is a complex sentence. Subordinate clauses cannot make sense by themselves and need to be linked to a main clause. They do the work of an adjective, an adverb or a noun in complex sentences, and are hence known as adjectival, adverbial and noun clauses.

The man *who* lives next door is my friend's brother-in-law.

The above complex sentence is formed by combining the simple sentences 'The man lives next door' and 'The man is my friend's brother-in-law.' However, although 'who lives next door' is a clause (called an adjectival or relative clause), it cannot stand on its own as an independent sentence. Look at some more examples of adjectival, adverbial and noun clauses. The italicised part of the sentence marks the subordinate clause, and the underlined word indicates the relative pronouns used to form complex sentences.

The email *<u>that</u> I sent Rita* bounced back. (adjectival clause)
The monkey scampered up the tree *<u>when</u> Keshav tried to touch* it. (adverbial clause)

Mother told us <u>*that*</u> *it was not safe to leave the doors open.* (noun clause)
The girl <u>*who*</u> *spoke to me at the dinner yesterday* is my classmate. (adjectival clause)
He shelled the peas <u>*while*</u> *listening to a music CD.* (adverbial clause)
<u>*What*</u> *you did* helped us. (noun clause)

It is thus possible to have, for example, any one of the following.

I sent Rita an email. It bounced back. (simple sentences)
or I sent Rita an email, but it bounced back. (compound sentence)
or The email that I sent Rita bounced back. (complex sentence)

You can form complex sentences (and recognise them too) by using subordinating conjunctions such as 'who', 'whose', 'which', 'that', 'when', 'while', 'where', 'before', 'after', 'since', 'till'/'until', 'as soon as', 'as'/'because'/'since', 'so that', 'if'/'unless', 'although'/'though', 'as though'/'as if', 'what', 'how' and 'whether'.

Exercise 3

Mark the following sentences as simple, compound or complex.

a. Janet is too weak to speak or move about.
b. Our company is taking in people who will work in the marketing division.
c. The flowers in the vase have wilted because of the heat.
d. Sujit has no experience as a teacher, yet the principal is willing to give him a chance.
e. The fruits in the glass bowl are for the guests.
f. On hearing about his father's arrival, Kamal rushed home.
g. It has been ages since I saw you.
h. This is the greatest satisfaction that an actor can hope for.

i. Sonal learnt glass painting while she was in Delhi.
j. The people trooped into the hall singing.

Exercise 4

Combine each of the following pairs of simple sentences into a complex sentence, using conjunctions of the type given above to change the second sentence into a subordinate clause. You can refer to the given example.

Varun showed me the old coins. Varun found the old coins in his garden.
Varun showed me the old coins that he found in his garden.

a. Varkey took me out to lunch. I went to see Varkey.
b. The woman put the bag down. The bag was very heavy.
c. I would like to read the poem. My son wrote a poem for his school magazine.
d. The doctor will be able to make an accurate diagnosis. Get the tests done.
e. The guavas are not sweet. The guavas are large.
f. It is our hope. The boy will grow up to be honest.
g. The lecture was very difficult. Maria could not understand it.
h. You cannot reach the fan. Stand on a stool.
i. Ben peeped into the room. His brothers were sleeping in the room.
j. It is my opinion. The room needs to be painted.

Exercise 5

Do as directed in the case of each of the following sentences.

a. Farid found the house locked, so he waited outside for his friend. (Change into a simple sentence.)
b. Even though we missed the bus, we got to office on time. (Change into a compound sentence.)
c. The squirrels hid the nuts at the usual place. (Change into a complex sentence.)
d. Although the curry was far too salty, Amit did not complain. (Change into a simple sentence.)

e. The nurses decorated the ward with flowers and balloons to make it look bright and cheerful.

(Change into a complex sentence.)

f. If you do not want to take the pink sari, you can take the white one. (Change into a compound sentence.)

g. Sitting under a shady tree, the family enjoyed their picnic lunch. (Change into a compound sentence.)

h. There was complete silence in the room, so Lily was able to concentrate. (Change into a complex sentence.)

i. The man who is wearing a white kurta speaks fluent Marathi. (Change into a simple sentence.)

j. You must return home before sunset. (Change into a complex sentence.)

2 Pronunciation

The Production of Speech

Before learning to produce the sounds that are used in English, let us quick look at the mechanism of speech. When speaking, the airstream coming out of the lungs is modified at different points and in many ways as it passes through the larynx, the pharynx, the mouth and the nasal cavity. You can locate the organs involved in the production of speech in the diagram below.

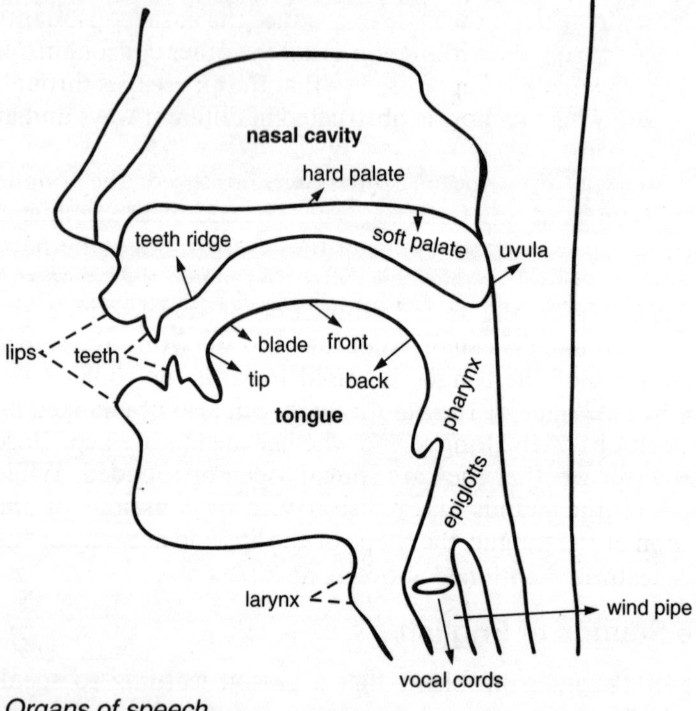

Organs of speech

First, the airstream moves up the wind pipe, or trachea, and passes through the larynx containing the vocal cords. The two vocal cords can be brought together or kept apart and the opening between them is called the glottis. When the vocal cords are kept close together, they vibrate when the air from the lungs passes between them through the narrowed glottis. This vibration produces voiced speech sounds, which include the vowels as well as some consonants such as /b, d, g, m, v, z/. Sounds produced when the vocal cords are kept fully apart are voiceless, such as the consonants /p, t, k, f, s/. You can feel the vibration and its absence if you place your fingers on the sides of your neck when producing, for example, the sounds /b/ and /p/. Further, the airstream is also modified in the pharynx, the mouth cavity and the nasal cavity. The roof of the mouth has three parts—the hard ridge (the alveolar ridge) just behind the upper teeth, the hard palate and the soft palate which ends in the uvula that can be lowered to allow air to pass only through the nose to produce the nasal consonants /m, n, ŋ/. During the production of all the other consonants in English, the uvula is kept raised so that the air escapes through the mouth where its flow is obstructed in different ways and at different points.

In studying how speech sounds are produced, the tongue can be seen as having three sections. The end of the tongue is called its tip. The parts opposite the alveolar ridge, the hard palate and the soft palate are called the blade, the front and the back respectively. In the production of vowel sounds, the tip of the tongue is usually kept low, and the front, the centre or the back of the tongue is raised towards the roof of the mouth. The shape of the mouth cavity can also be changed by the positions of the tongue and whether the lips are kept close together or whether they are spread, open or rounded. While practising the sounds of English, try to be conscious of the position of the tongue, the shape of the lips and as many of the other features mentioned above as possible.

The Sounds of English

One of the main problems that a person learning to speak English often faces is that of pronunciation. Mastering English pronunciation will mean learning how to produce its sounds and also understanding how these combine to form words and sentences in speech. Second language learners, whose mother tongues are the different Indian languages, find some of the sounds of English easy to pronounce—those that are used in their own languages. Thus, speakers of Hindi, Malayalam, Assamese or Marathi, will have no problems with sounds such as /p/, /g/ and /k/ in the words 'apart', girl' and 'actor'. However, these persons may find it a little difficult to learn to pronounce the sounds /ɔː/, /θ/ and /ð/ in the words 'caught', 'thin' and 'that'. This is because the sounds concerned are not present in their mother tongues and have to be learnt as 'new' sounds. It is therefore important when learning spoken English to learn, firstly, how to produce the sounds of the language and, secondly, also how to say individual words as well as complete sentences fluently. Note though that several internationally recognised varieties of English are spoken in the world today by large numbers of people, and Indian English is prominent among these. It is hence argued that it is not really essential that we perfect standard British English. As second-language learners, it is enough if we aim to speak Standard Indian English which is internationally intelligible. In spite of this argument, it is best to begin learning spoken English by practising the sounds of standard British English. This will help you understand and communicate with English speaking people from other countries.

The sounds of English, as of other languages, can be grouped into consonants and vowels. Look at the list of 44 consonants and vowels in English and the phonetic symbols used to represent them. Each vowel and consonant in the list is accompanied by a set of words containing the sound concerned. For practice, say aloud, first the sounds, and then the words given as examples. Your teacher will help you practise the sounds that are you are not familiar with. Note how the sounds appear in different positions in words—the beginning, middle and end of words. Read them as many times as you can and practise saying them in pairs and also individually.

CONSONANTS

Consonant sounds are sounds in the production of which there is either a closure or a narrowing of the air passage in the mouth cavity. In producing consonant sounds, therefore, the air flow from the lungs is either stopped very briefly in the mouth cavity before being released (e.g., the sound /p/ in 'pin') or is allowed to pass through a narrowed passage, causing friction that can be heard (e.g., the sound /s/ in 'silk'). There are twenty-four different consonants in English. First, consonants can be identified as *voiced* (e.g., /b, d, g/) and *voiceless* (e.g., /p, t, k/, depending on whether the vocal cords vibrate or not when air passes through them. Secondly, these can be classified according to their *place of articulation* in the mouth, which is the point inside the mouth where they are produced (for e.g., bilabial if articulated by the two lips coming together as in /p, b, m, w/, dental if produced by the tip of the tongue against the upper teeth as in /θ, ð/, velar if produced by the back of the tongue against the soft palate as in /k, g, ŋ/, etc). Thirdly, the consonants in English can be classified according to their *manner of articulation*, which tells us how they are produced (for e.g., plosive if the air stream is stopped briefly and then released as in /p, t, k/, nasal if there is a complete closure of the air passage in the mouth and the air escapes through the nose as in /m, n, ŋ/, fricative if the air escapes through a narrow passage in the mouth causing friction and a hissing sound as in /f, v, s, z/, etc).

The following chart will show you how the consonants in English are classified. Also given is a list of the 24 consonants together with some examples of the words they appear in. You can refer to the chart when practising these sounds.

/p/: page, pet, pen, purse, apple, upper, helicopter, captain, tape, map, cap, cape

/b/: bat, box, bin, bed, but, break, blue, about, laboratory, sober, tub, cub

/t/: toy, tin, test, tell, caterpillar, attract, attend, pattern, cat, sat, late, kit

Classification of English consonants

Place →	bilabial		labio-dental		dental		alveolar		post-alveolar	palato-alveolar		palatal	velar		glottal
Manner ↓	vl	vd	vl	vd	vl	vd	vl	vd	vd	vl	vd	vd	vl	vd	vl
plosive	**p**	**b**					**t**	**d**					**k**	**g**	
affricate										**tʃ**	**dʒ**				
fricative			**f**	**v**	**θ**	**ð**	**s**	**z**		**ʃ**	**ʒ**				**h**
nasal		**m**						**n**						**ŋ**	
lateral								**l**							
glide (semi-vowel)		**w**							**r**			**j**			

/**d**/: desk, den, doll, dress, adapt, adore, ladder, teddy, lead, toad, paid, said

/**k**/: kid, kitchen, kettle, kind, king, liquor, wicket, mosquito, luck, block, lock, pick

/**g**/: gold, great, girl, goat, again, begin, argue, luggage, tug, pig, leg, plague

/**tʃ**/: chin, church, chill, check, chat, chicken, actual, pitcher, ketchup, nature, lunch, catch

/**dʒ**/: jam, jelly, jail, gentle, jacket, agile, bridge, suggest, soldier, judge, lodge, fridge

/**f**/: feel, fall, finger, first, afraid, laughter, safety, typhoon, tough, cough, life, safe

/**v**/: velocity, vain, victory, visit, liver, never, clever, reverse, live, love, leave, brave

/**θ**/: thin, thirst, thrust, third, think, thing, thunder, bath, both, mouth, mathematics, faith

/**ð**/: this, that, them, there, then, though, father, mother, rather, either, neither, bathe

/**s**/: sit, sell, cell, scent, assert, ask, fast, missed, bus, pass, lace, nice

/**z**/: zest, zone, zoo, zero, zinc, desire, reason, busy, lose, leaves, hives, birds

/**ʃ**/: sheep, sheet, shell, shout, fashion, lotion, ashes, portion, cash, polish, wish, bush

/ʒ/: pleasure, leisure, measure, treasure, erosion, division, rouge, beige, mirage

/h/: he, hot, hill, heavy, hen, huge, behind, perhaps, cowherd, hardly

/m/: mother, mind, mill, master, harmful, temple, fumble, formula, tame, team, atom, loom

/n/: nurse, never, not, neat, tent, deny, bend, lantern, ten, cushion, brown, sign

/ŋ/: finger, trunk, singer, uncle, bring, sing, long, among, rung

/l/: lid, lead, list, lemon, split, flame, pillar, filler, silly, ball, feel, tell

/r/: rat, roll, ribbon, write, shrine, front, carry, train, bread, run, carrot, rose

/j/: you, yell, yellow, university, union, youth, few, huge, beautiful, queue, due, pupil

/w/: water, well, winter, one, what, why, switch, reward, dwelling, dwarf, always, squeeze

Vowels

In producing vowel sounds, there is no closure or narrowing made at any point in the mouth cavity. Thus, vowel sounds are produced when the air from the lungs comes out in a continuous stream, and the vocal cords vibrate to produce 'voice'. The production of different vowels in English depends fully on the degree of raising of the tongue (without causing friction or a closure), on the part of the tongue that is raised and on whether the lips are kept spread, open or rounded. Thus, vowels are classified as close (when the tongue is as close as possible to the roof of the mouth), half-close, half-open and open as in /iː, e, æ, ʌ/. Further, in the front vowels /iː, i, e, æ, ʌ/, the highest part of the tongue is its front while in the back vowels /ɑː, ɒ, ɔː, ʊ, uː/ it is the back of the tongue. When the centre of the tongue is raised to the highest degree in the mouth, we have the central vowels /ɜː, ə/. The classification is shown graphically in the diagram on the next page.

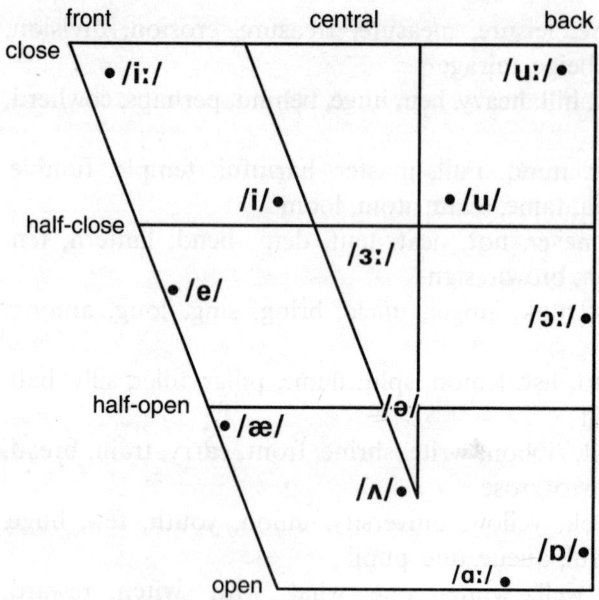

Tongue positions for vowels

Pure vowels

If the quality of a vowel does not change, it is called a pure vowel. English has 12 pure vowels which are given below together with some examples of the words they appear in.

/iː/: keep, these, feet, leave, sieve, free, tea, key, me, seat, meek, breed

/ɪ/: sit, lip, wick, nib, tin, imitate, politics, refrigerator, remember, military

/e/: bed, bread, fell, rest, bend, any, general, every, treasure, leisure

/æ/: fat, bad, rack, flag, map, cattle, mango, attack, matter, gratitude

/ʌ/: blood, bun, pus, butter, enough, country, couple, study, trouble, cup

/ɑː/: card, arm, large, car, harm, half, part, father, alarm, disaster

/ɒ/: hot, not, box, off, top, bottle, honest, model, revolve, follow
/ɔː/: horse, all, bought, force, ball, law, cause, walk, talk, crawl
/ʊ/: book, took, look, should, wood, put, butcher, bullet, crooked, full
/uː/: loom, groove, tube, rule, fume, fool, approve, music, bruises, movement
/ɜː/: girl, bird, journey, burn, learn, turn, word, perfect, worse, curtain
/ə/: account, about, human, doctor, connect, ribbon, mother, ten, enter, elder

Diphthongs

Diphthongs are produced when there is a smooth glide from one vowel to another within the same syllable. English has the following 8 diphthongs. Practise these by saying the words given along with each aloud. As diphthongs do not occur in Indian languages, take the help of your teacher in learning to produce these.

/eɪ/: male, gate, take, fate, baker, grate, rate, shape, sail, make
/aɪ/: bite, die, five, side, tiger, pilot, bright, while, fight, sign
/ɔɪ/: boy, toil, loiter, joy, moisture, noise, coin, employ, join, spoil
/əʊ/: home, float, close, bone, boat, port, ocean, loaf, note, soak
/ɑʊ/: vowel, down, doubt, loud, shout, howl, devour, cow, around, bow
/ɪə/: tear, cheer, dear, hear, here, career, clear, severe, spear, peer
/eə/: air, fair, there, wear, scarce, affair, stair, care, tear, mare
/ʊə/: tour, poor, sure, fuel, fewer, lure, sewer, cruel, gruel

Phonetic Transcription

It is not possible to exactly represent speech sounds with letters of the alphabet because the letters do not always correspond with the sounds in the language. (For example, the letter 'a' can represent the sounds /ɑː/, /æ/, /eɪ/ or /ʌ/.) To identify sounds, we make use of a different system of written symbols called the International Phonetic Alphabet (IPA). While some of the IPA symbols are the letters of the English alphabet, there are other special symbols as well.

You would have noticed that dictionaries give the pronunciation of every word, using phonetic symbols. This kind of exact representation of the pronunciation of words is called phonetic transcription, which could be a useful tool in learning to pronounce words correctly. As examples, some words and their phonetic transcriptions are given below. Look at these and practise saying the words aloud.

word	phonetic transcription	word	phonetic transcription
gain	**/geɪn/**	keep	**/kiːp/**
short	**/ʃɔːt/**	learn	**/lɜːn/**
vote	**/vəʊt/**	mail	**/meɪl/**
coil	**/kɔɪl/**	need	**/niːd/**
find	**/faɪnd/**	oar	**/ɔː/**
thought	**/θɔːt/**	paste	**/peɪst/**
harm	**/hɑːm/**	quench	**/kwentʃ/**
gem	**/dʒem/**	run	**/rʌn/**
class	**/klɑːs/**	scrap	**/skræp/**
phone	**/fəʊn/**	truth	**/truːθ/**
teach	**/tiːtʃ/**	use (verb)	**/juːz/**
faith	**/feɪθ/**	use (noun)	**/juːs/**
ache	**/eɪk/**	vague	**/veɪg/**
bark	**/bɑːk/**	what	**/wɒt/**
cancel	**/kænsəl/**	yacht	**/jɒt/**
debt	**/det/**	zinc	**/zɪŋk/**
easy	**/iːzi/**	arm	**/ɑːm/**
fair	**/feə/**	beach	**/biːtʃ/**
gasp	**/gɑːsp/**	bridge	**/brɪdʒ/**
hang	**/hæŋ/**	clause	**/klɔːz/**
ice	**/aɪs/**	down	**/daʊn/**
joke	**/dʒəʊk/**	each	**/iːtʃ/**

word	**phonetic transcription**	**word**	**phonetic transcription**
floor	**/flɔ:/**	job	**/dʒɒb/**
goal	**/gəʊl/**	knife	**/naɪf/**
hear	**/hɪə/**	leap	**/li:p/**
heir	**/eə/**	mole	**/məʊl/**
jam	**/dʒæm/**	nose	**/nəʊz/**
know	**/nəʊ/**	oil	**/ɔɪl/**
launch	**/lɔ:ntʃ/**	pay	**/peɪ/**
map	**/mæp/**	queen	**/kwi:n/**
nerve	**/nɜ:v/**	rash	**/ræʃ/**
opt	**/ɒpt/**	sun	**/sʌn/**
pipe	**/paɪp/**	task	**/tɑ:sk/**
quest	**/kwest/**	urge	**/ɜ:dʒ/**
quartz	**/kwɔ:ts/**	vase	**/vɑ:z/**
range	**/reɪndʒ/**	weave	**/wi:v/**
scarf	**/skɑ:f/**	yard	**/ja:d/**
tame	**/teɪm/**	zone	**/zəʊn/**
van	**/væn/**	smile	**/smaɪl/**
walk	**/wɔ:k/**	church	**/tʃɜ:tʃ/**
yield	**/ji:ld/**	flight	**/flaɪt/**
zip	**/zɪp/**	heap	**/hi:p/**
arch	**/ɑ:tʃ/**	pull	**/pʊl/**
ball	**/bɔ:l/**	snake	**/sneɪk/**
calf	**/kɑ:f/**	sport	**/spɔ:t/**
dare	**/deə/**	gold	**/gəʊld/**
end	**/end/**	phrase	**/freɪz/**
filth	**/fɪlθ/**	rear	**/rɪə/**
gym	**/dʒɪm/**	fun	**/fʌn/**
halt	**/hɔ:lt/**	play	**/pleɪ/**
iron	**/aɪən/**		

Exercise

Write the phonetic transcriptions for the following words. Working in pairs, use a dictionary to check your answers. Practise saying the words aloud.

a. zoo
b. dead
c. show
d. lot
e. soak
f. cane
g. chair
h. paw
i. flower
j. paint
k. fish
l. arc
m. bake
n. call
o. dash
p. ever
q. gas
r. bowl
s. tall
t. hand
u. knee
v. leak
w. moist
x. note
y. one
z. three

Stress

Stress, or accent, is an important feature of English, and clarity in the language depends to a large extent on the speaker's ability to use the English stress system. Stress is a means of making a syllable or a word appear more prominent than others to which it is linked in speech. The three signals of stress in English are:

- loudness (or greater breath force)
- length of the vowel in a syllable
- pitch change

Stress is a meaningful feature at the levels of both words and sentences.

Word stress

The articulation of words in English gives prominence to one or more syllables in them. (A syllable is a unit of sound consisting of a vowel and/or one or more consonant sounds that can be produced in one effort. For example, 'tea' is monosyllabic, 'coffee' is disyllabic and 'camera' is trisyllabic.) This prominence is called word stress. Monosyllabic words, consisting of one syllable, when uttered in isolation, are spoken with force, but in a word consisting of two syllables either the first or the second or both the syllables are stressed. All the syllables in a multi-syllabic word do not have the same degree of stress. For example, 'teacher' is a two-syllable word with the first syllable louder than the second. The vowel in the first syllable, which is stressed, is also longer than in the second syllable. In dictionaries, a vertical bar /ˈ/ is placed above and in front of the syllable that carries the *primary stress* (or the main stress) of the word. For example, the words 'teacher' and 'letter' would be marked for stress as *ˈteach.er* and *ˈlet.ter*. Some words also have *secondary stress* (a weaker stress) on another syllable. The vertical bar /ˌ/ is usually placed below and in front of a syllable with a weaker stress. For example, 'misspell' will be marked for accent as *ˌmis.ˈspell*—with the secondary stress placed before the first syllable and the primary stress before the second. However, at this stage you need to learn only about the placement of primary stress. The first problem that a learner of English faces is the seemingly irregular ways in which the syllables are accented in disyllabic and polysyllabic words. Let us look at a few examples.

Stress in disyllabic words

In words with two or more syllables, it is often difficult to say which syllable is the loudest, or which receives the primary stress. Some disyllabic words, like *ˈsingle*, *ˈmother* and *ˈheaven*, receive the primary stress on the first syllable, while other disyllabic words, like *aˈgain*, *reˈmark* and *hoˈtel*, have the main stress on the second syllable.

Look at the following examples of how disyllabic words are stressed. In each case, listen to your teacher pronounce the word and repeat it, placing the stress on the right syllable.

Stress on the first syllable

ˈEng.lish	ˈa.ble	ˈdoc.tor	ˈbag.gage
ˈpri.vate	ˈcap.tain	ˈla.zy	ˈdam.age
ˈpa.tient	ˈea.ger	ˈbis.cuit	ˈac.tor
ˈad.verb	ˈan.gry	ˈcar.ton	ˈcei.ling
ˈda.ta	ˈde.cent	ˈen.gine	ˈfro.zen

'gath.er	'har.vest	'i.tem	'jack.et
'jeal.ous	'kid.ney	'la.bour	'lim.it
'man.y	'mar.ket	'na.tion	'neigh.bour
'o.pen	'o.ral	'ped.al	'pep.per
'quar.rel	'rain.y	'scrib.ble	'trol.ley

Stress on the second syllable

ad.'dress	a.'bout	de.'sign	be.'cause
pre.'tend	ca.'nal	de.'mand	de.'ceive
pre.'vent	ef.'fect	im.'pose	en.'rol
be.'come	con.'sult	con.'tain	ex.'cept
ex.'pand	gi.'raffe	i.'deal	in.'crease
ne.'glect	ob.'tain	oc.'cur	re.'ceive
re.'late	re.'lax	re.'mind	sham.'poo
trans.'late	un.'fit	de.'light	de.'sire
de.'pend	pos.'sess	pre.'dict	u.'nite
in.'clude	as.'sist	a.'gain	a.'larm

Stress on both syllables

'fif.'teen
'non.'sense

Exercise 1

Refer to a dictionary and place the accent in front of the right syllable in the following words. Then say each word aloud, taking care to stress the marked syllable.

a. tackle	k. collar
b. driver	l. dentist
c. village	m. master
d. welcome	n. package
e. permit (v)	o. nightmare
f. allot	p. untrue
g. devote	q. beside
h. ignore	r. recourse
i. pretext	s. imply
j. defect	t. allow

Stress in polysyllabic words

Stress in polysyllabic words varies considerably. There are trisyllabic words like *ˈpermanent*, *ˈregister*, *ˈinterval*, which receive the accent on the first syllable, but in other trisyllabic words like *perˈmission*, *reˈflection*, *deˈvelop*, the accent is placed on the second syllable or on the third syllable, as in words like *cigaˈrette*, *disapˈpoint* and *underˈstand*. In polysyllabic words with prefixes and suffixes, the stem part of the word, which is more important from the point of view of meaning, is always stressed, while prefixes and suffixes (except the negative markers) are not. However, each word should be treated independently.

Listen to your teacher pronounce the following words and repeat them, placing stress on the right syllables.

oc.ˈca.sion	dis.con.ˈnect
re.ˈac.tor	fa.ˈmi.liar
im.ˈpos.si.ble	dis.em.ˈbark
sul.ˈphur.ic	des.ˈcrib.ing
in.ˈfla.tion	half.ˈfi.nished
fi.ˈnan.cial	in.ex.ˈpe.ri.enced
pro.ˈduc.tion	in.sin.ˈcere
de.ˈpen.dent	il.ˈlo.gi.cal

Exercise 2

Refer to a dictionary and place the accent in front of the right syllable in the following words. Then say each word aloud, taking care to stress the marked syllable.

a. professor	g. horizon
b. calculate	h. ambition
c. important	i. delicate
d. educate	j. recognise
e. promotion	k. engineer
f. deliver	l. committee

Stress shift in derived words

Another difficulty faced by the non-native speaker of English has to do with the change in the accented syllables of derived words. Some typical examples are given below. There are of course some exceptions to such shifts in stress, e.g., *conˈclude*, *conˈclusive*, *conˈclusion* in which the derived words have the accent on the same syllable as the main word.

Listen to your teacher pronounce the following words and repeat them, placing stress on the right syllables.

ˈdemocrat (primary accent on the first syllable)
deˈmocracy (primary accent on the second syllable)
demoˈcratic (primary accent on the third syllable)
ˈdemonstrate (primary accent on the first syllable)
deˈmonstrative (primary accent on the second syllable)
demonˈstration (primary accent on the third syllable)
ˈphotograph (primary accent on the first syllable)
phoˈtographer (primary accent on the second syllable)
photoˈgraphic (primary accent on the third syllable)

Exercise 3

Refer to a dictionary and place the accent in front of the right syllable in the following words. Then say each word aloud, taking care to stress the marked syllable.

a. academy
b. academic
c. academician
d. bacteria
e. bacteriology
f. bacteriological
g. individual
h. individuality
i. individualistic
j. politics
k. political
l. politician

Stress shift according to function

Another aspect of English word stress concerns shift in accent in a number of disyllabic words, depending on whether the words are used as nouns, as adjectives or as verbs. Usually, nouns or adjectives receive the accent on the first syllable, and when the same words are used as verbs, the accent falls on the second syllable. (There are also some exceptions to this rule for not all disyllabic nouns and verbs undergo such a shift in the accented syllable. For example, in words like *ˈor.der*, *re.ˈform*, *ˈvi.sit* and *ad.ˈvance*, the primary stress is on the same syllable whether they are used as nouns or as verbs.) Listen to your teacher pronounce the following words and practise saying them, placing stress on the right syllables.

noun/adjective	**verb**
ˈdesert	deˈsert
ˈsurvey	surˈvey
ˈpermit	perˈmit
ˈpresent	preˈsent
ˈperfect	perˈfect
ˈobject	obˈject
ˈexport	exˈport
ˈimport	imˈport
ˈrebel	reˈbel

Exercise 4

Refer to a dictionary and place the accent in front of the right syllable in the following words. Then say each word aloud, taking care to stress the marked syllable.

noun/adjective	**verb**
a. produce	g. produce
b. progress	h. progress
c. record	i. record
d. subject	j. subject
e. increase	k. increase
f. defeat	l. defeat

Stress in compound words

In a compound word, consisting of a combination of two words, the primary accent is generally on one element—usually the first.

Sometimes both elements are accented, but then the primary accent is on the second element.

Listen to your teacher pronounce the following words and practise saying them, placing stress on the right syllables.

primary accent on the first element	**primary accent on the second element**
ˈblack.board	part.ˈtime
ˈrain.coat	short.ˈlived
ˈrail.way	four.ˈfooted
ˈstone.age	down.ˈhearted
ˈmotor.car	open.ˈminded
ˈgreen.house	middle.ˈclass
ˈbook.shelf	loud.ˈspeaker

Exercise 5

Refer to a dictionary and place the accent in front of the right syllable in the following words. Then say each word aloud, taking care to stress the marked syllable.

a. teabag	g. hot tempered
b. waterproof	h. afternoon
c. wholesale	i. halfway
d. anything	j. middle-aged
e. backbone	k. north-west
f. earthquake	l. goldsmith

SENTENCE STRESS

Not all the words in a sentence are stressed. Content words, which are vital to meaning, such as nouns, verbs, adjectives and adverbs generally get the stress while pronouns and grammatical words like helping verbs, prepositions, articles and conjunctions are not stressed. This is because being few in number and also used very frequently, the listener can get the meaning of the sentence even without hearing these words clearly. Let us take a few sentences and mark the words that stand out from the rest.

He has 'gone.
I 'met him in the 'morning.
It's an 'hour's 'journey from 'here.
I 'like 'studying 'English.
He 'lost his 'keys in the 'bus.
'This is the 'car that 'Shailesh 'bought.
'Did you 'meet my 'friend 'John?
I shall 'see you 'later.
'Where does he 'live?
I 'usually 'watch 'T.V. before 'going to 'bed.

As a general rule, the words which carry the main information in a sentence stand out from the rest. For example, in a sentence like, 'He wants to buy a camera', the words 'wants', 'buy' and 'camera' are more prominent than the other words 'he', 'to', 'a'. But it is important to realise that when we place a sentence in the context of a conversation or a speech situation, any word can be given the primary accent in a sentence. This shift in the primary accent placed on words in a sentence has the effect of changing its meaning to suit different speech situations. For example, the following sentences can be spoken in different ways to convey different meanings.

'That is Ravi's sister. (not the other one)
That 'is Ravi's sister. (confirming)
That is 'Ravi's sister. (not Hari's)
That is Ravi's 'sister. (not his niece)

I like boiled 'eggs. (not potatoes)
I like 'boiled eggs. (not fried)
I 'like boiled eggs. (do not dislike them)
'I like boiled eggs. (especially I)

The accent patterns illustrated above show how important it is to stress the correct word in a spoken sentence. We also see that in English connected speech, the accented and unaccented syllables follow each other in a regular pattern. English, for the reason, is said to have a stress-timed rhythm where the strong or accented syllables occur at regular intervals of time. The number of weak or unaccented syllables that can occur between the accented ones, however, may vary. Look at the following examples.

'Prem has 'just re'turned from 'Jhansi.
My 'brother has been 'training 'hard for the 'sports 'day.

In the first sentence above, there is one unaccented syllable between two accented ones. Thus, *'Prem*, *'just*, *'turned* (of the word 'returned') and *'Jhan* (of the word 'Jhansi') occur at regular intervals. In the second sentence, there are three unaccented syllables between *'bro* (of the word 'brother') and *'train* (of the word 'training'), one between *'train* and *'hard*, two between *'hard* and *'sports*, and none between *'sports* and *'day*. Such distribution of accented and unaccented syllables is a very important feature of spoken English. The rhythm of English connected speech require us to pronounce the accented syllables clearly, and the unaccented syllables are spoken rapidly, specially if there are too many of them. Roughly speaking, the time taken to pronounce two, three or more unaccented syllables would be the same.

Strong and weak forms

As said above, the unaccented words between the accented ones in informal speech at a natural pace are spoken rapidly. Consequently these words have two forms–strong forms, as pronounced when the words are uttered individually, and weak forms that are reduced when these words are uttered in connected speech. This reduction is mainly a result of the weakening of the vowel(s) in a word. For example, the word 'would', pronounced in isolation as /wud/, is often reduced to /əd/ or /d/. Thus, words like articles, auxiliary verbs, conjunctions and prepositions do not usually appear as strong forms in conversational speech. Many people in India for whom English is a second language speak as they would write—using strong forms instead of the weak forms that will occur in the speech of native speakers of English. Look at some examples of strong and weak forms of words that are unaccented in speech.

word	strong form	weak form	example of use
articles			
a	/ai/	/ə/	a book
an	/æn/	/ðɪ/	an egg
the	/ði:/	/di/ (before a vowel)	the army
		/ðə/ (before a consonant)	the pencil
aux. verbs			
am	/æm/	/əm, m/	I'm a student.
are	/ɑ:/	/ə/	They're friendly.
is	/iz/	/z, s/	He's my brother. It's a nice day.
was	/wɒ/	/wəz/	I was happy.
will	/wil/	/l/	You'll do well.
conjunctions			
and	/ænd/	/ənd, ən/	bread and butter
that	/ðæt/	/ðət/	Joy knows that she is here.
prepositions			
at	/æt/	/ət/	Look at this.
for	/fɔ:/	/fə/	They came for help.
from	/frɒm/	/frəm/	I'm from Sri Lanka.
to	/tu:/	/tə/ before consonants	We're going to Munnar.
		/tu/ before vowels	It is ten to eight.
of	/ɑv/	/əv/	a box of sweets

Exercise 6

Mark the stressed words in the following sentences.

a. I parked the car by the side of the building.

b. The dog jumped into the stream.

c. She is making a dress for Naina.
d. Your classes start from Thursday.
e. Giri said that he was tired.
f. The trees in the forest caught fire.
g. Valsan is my cousin.
h. Give the wooden box to the man in the white shirt.
i. The glass needs to be wiped.
j. This is a government document.

Intonation

The pitch at which stressed syllables are uttered in natural speech can be high, low or it can change from high to low or low to high. Any change in the pitch of accented syllables in spoken sentences is known as intonation or tone. Like stress, intonation is a very meaningful feature of English, that every second language learner will need practice in. This is because intonation indicates the sentence type (e.g., statement or question) as well as the attitude of the speaker. The main intonation patterns in English are: the falling tone, the rising tone and the falling-rising tone.

FALLING TONE

A falling tone is marked by the symbol [ˋ]in front of the accented syllable where the change in pitch begins. It is used in making ordinary statements as in the sentences below.

We're late for ˋoffice.
The child is ˋhungry.
Mother is sending an ˋemail.
I live in an ˋapartment.
It is six o'ˋclock.
The sea is rough ˋtoday.

The falling tone is also used in commands and in questions beginning with the words 'what', 'why', 'where', 'when', 'which' and 'how', asked to seek some information. For examples of this, look at the sentences below.

Open the ˋdoor.
Stop the ˋcar.
Give her the ˋmoney.
What is your ˋname?
Why did you ˋleave?
Where is the ˋspoon?
When will Nikhil ˋreturn?
Which book did she ˋchoose?
How is the ˋpatient?

Question tags take a falling tone when they are used to seek agreement.

You are my friend, ˋaren't you? (The speaker is sure of what she is saying.)

Rising tone

A rising tone is marked by the symbol [ˊ]in front of the accented syllable where the change in pitch begins. It is used firstly in questions which seek a yes–no answer.

Is the waterˊcool?
Are you ˊcoming?
Was the film ˊgood?
Do they speak ˊTelugu?
Has she bought a ˊcar?
Will you water the ˊplants?

(Note that the rising tone is sometimes used in interrogative sentences with question words like 'how' and 'what'. This is done to convey a sense of warmth or friendliness as, for example, in 'What is the ˊmatter?')

The rising tone is also used to make polite requests.

Could you explain this, ˊplease.
Please come to the ˊparty.
Would you drop me ˊhome.

Question tags take a rising tone when used to seek confirmation.

The man has left, ˊhasn't he? (The speaker is not sure he is right.)

Finally, the rising tone is used to convey sarcasm.

The man is ˊpowerful. (and, for example, can do as he pleases)
The earth is ours to ˊpollute. (when it is not really so)

FALLING-RISING TONE

A falling-rising tone is marked by the symbol [ˇ] placed in front of the accented syllable(s) concerned. It is used to convey more than the literal meaning of the sentence and these implied meanings are the speaker's attitudes such as doubt, sarcasm, reassurance and apology. Examples are given below.

The situation is not ˇcompletely bad. (reassuring)
The cook can surely make us a ˇcup of coffee. (sarcastic)
You can ˇmanage. (doubtful)
Although we lost the order, I ˇdid try hard. (apologetic)

Exercise

Say whether the following sentences will be said with a falling, rising or falling-rising tone. Place the intonation marks in front of the appropriate syllables.

a. Good morning.
b. Where will you stay?
c. This is a jackfruit.
d. Ashwin has applied for a job.
e. Were the soldiers safe?
f. Did Bill find his keys?
g. What a surprise!
h. When did you move to Pathankot?
i. Harish is a lawyer.
j. The house is nearly complete. (Not to worry for it will be ready shortly.)

3 Reading Comprehension

Today, much of the available knowledge in the world is to be found in books and periodicals published in the English language. In recent years, the Internet has also become a valuable source of knowledge, and the language of the Internet is mainly English. It is important for everyone, but particularly for students, to be able to access this knowledge which is available in printed or in written form in English. This is possible only if the skills of reading are developed.

To improve your reading skills, you must read different kinds of English texts independently and try to understand them. By the word 'text' we mean here any piece of language, in printed or in written form, which has some meaning that the reader can 'recover' through the process of reading. A text may be an article, or a part of an article, an essay, a story or a report published in a newspaper, a magazine or a book. The minimum length of a text is usually a paragraph containing several sentences, but a text can be shorter or longer.

Students who come out of schools often develop the habit of reading aloud. When children first learn to read—that is, to recognise the letters of the alphabet as well as small words in print—it is useful to make them read out aloud. But once a student reaches the high school or the college level, the process of reading should become silent. Readers should only use their eyes while reading, and not their voices. A good reader should be able to read at a speed of at least 300 words per minute, whereas if one reads aloud, one cannot reach a speed of more than 100 words a minute. Since most educated people have to read large amounts of 'text' (books, magazines, newspapers, legal documents, etc.) every day, developing an acceptable 'reading speed' is very necessary.

We read in order to understand the ideas that the writer is trying to convey to us through the words in the text. Very often a writer has one central, or main idea, which is developed in different ways. Sometimes, however, the text may contain other ideas which are not related to the main idea. The most important skill required for reading is the ability to recognise the central idea, separating it from other less significant ideas.

You may find that the main idea is repeated several times (in different ways), when the writer thinks that it is very important and that the reader may miss it if it is not repeated. You must also be able to recognise these repetitions of the central idea. It is also necessary to understand how this central idea is developed in a text. Often, the writer gives instances to support a general statement. Here is an example.

> A lot of development has taken place in this village during the last five years. A new road has been built, and three schools have been opened. A new hospital has also come up.

Here, the second and third sentences provide supporting examples of the 'development' that is mentioned in the opening sentence.

Look at another example of a text in which the main idea is developed in a different way.

> You must develop the skill of reading. If you do not, you will miss a lot of interesting news which is published in newspapers.

Here, the second sentence provides an argument, or reason, in support of the opening sentence. So another important skill that you need in order to be able to read well is the ability to understand how the main idea of the text is developed.

The skills of reading, like the skills of listening, speaking and writing can only be developed through practice. The more you read, the better you will become as a reader. In this chapter, we provide a few passages for you to read and understand independently. After you have read each passage, go through the exercises that have been provided. The purpose of these exercises is to help you to understand the texts, and thereby to develop the skills of reading.

We are sure you will find these texts interesting, as they deal with subjects that you are familiar with already.

1

Read through the passage below and answer the questions that follow.

Welcome to 'God's own country'! One of India's most beautiful states, Kerala, is an *exotic cocktail* of the very best that nature can offer. Soak in the flavours of this *tropical paradise,* among the beauty of pencil-slim coconut palms, where the flowers are specially bright and their fragrance specially strong. When God created Kerala, He wanted it to be remembered as a land of *abundance*. So, there are tons of coconuts and cashew, heaps of spices and generous amounts of fish. Add to that a generous *sprinkling* of rivers, mountains and some of the world's finest beaches. What you get is a land of natural wonders that attracts visitors from all over the world.

Kerala is just the place for you if you love variety. There is something here to please everyone. You are sure to fall in love with the *serene* beauty of Kerala's magical backwaters. When you have experienced that, you can *sample* the excitement of Kerala's *bustling* cities, or retreat into the villages to see at first-hand how time can stand still. Better still, take a trip to the spice gardens in the hills, to *inhale* the fragrance of fresh cardamoms. If that makes your tastebuds *tingle* and fills you with dreams of food, you need not worry. Kerala's *cuisine* is known for its spicy, hot flavours. The coconut and the spices give the food—especially the seafood—a *pungency* that is *enhanced* by tamarind. Your meal would be incomplete without appam, rasam, fish curry and some delicious payasam. To wash it down, sip the naturally refreshing water of a tender coconut. And, when you have had your fill, move into the markets to shop for gold, handicrafts, spices, cashewnuts and coffee. Bargain-hunters will never have a problem since English is spoken and understood everywhere in Kerala.

Unfamiliar words

Study the meanings of the following words which appear in the passage. Then read the passage again, trying to relate the meanings of the words to the contexts.

exotic cocktail : an unusual and surprising mixture of several different items

tropical paradise : a warm, wet place, not far from the equator, which is full of natural wonders, specially many kinds of plants and animals

abundance : a great quantity; pleanty

sprinkling (noun) : a small quantity of something which is added to food, etc. to improve its taste, e.g., a sprinkling of salt in a curry

serene (adjective) : calm and peaceful

sample (verb) : to form an idea or impression of something by examining only a very small quantity of it, e.g., to sample a curry by tasting only one spoonful of it

bustling (adj.) : busy and crowded

inhale : to breathe in

tingle (verb) : to create a mild and pleasant feeling of excitement

cuisine (noun) : the style of cooking which is found in a particular place

pungency (noun) : strong taste, e.g., the pungency of green chillies

enhance (verb) : to increase; to make something better

Comprehension questions

1. What is the other name used for Kerala in this passage? Can you figure out the reason for this from the passage?
2. Why is Kerala described as a land of abundance?
3. What is special about the food that one finds in Kerala?
4. Why does the writer say that foreigners visiting Kerala will have no problems there?
5. What are some of the attractions of Kerala that the writer of this passage mentions? Can you make a list of at least five of them?
6. From which source do you think has this passage been taken? Why do you think so?

Vocabulary

Fill in the blanks in the sentences below, using appropriate words from the given list. (Use verbs in their correct tense forms.)

1. There is an .... of fish in this lake.
2. The beauty of her face was .... by her long, dark hair.
3. You should not .... the harmful gases produced by motor cars.
4. If you are a lover of Chinese .... , you should visit this restaurant.
5. He spoke in Malayalam but used a .... of English words.

tingle, inhale, bustling, sprinkling, pungency, abundance, cuisine, enhance

2

Read through the passage below and answer the questions that follow.

Arundhati Roy, the famous novelist and *activist,* who won the Booker Prize in 1997 for her novel, 'The God of Small Things', was born in Shillong, Meghalaya, on November 24, 1961, to a Keralite mother and a Bengali father. She spent her childhood in Aymanam, in Kerala, with her mother. Arundhati left Kerala for Delhi at the age of 16 and *embarked on* a *bohemian lifestyle,* staying in a small hut with a tin roof and making a living by selling empty bottles. She studied architecture in Delhi but did not take it up as a profession.

In 1984, Arundhati began a brief career in films, under the influence of her husband, who was a film-maker. She played the role of a village girl in the award-winning movie 'Massey Sahib' and also wrote the screenplay for the film 'In Which Annie Gives it Those Ones'.

Roy began writing 'The God of Small Things' in 1992 and finished it in 1996. She received half-a-million pounds (about Rs 3.5 crore) as an advance from the publishers, and the rights to the book were sold in twenty-one countries. The book is semi-autobiographical and a major part of it captures her childhood in Aymanam.

When India tested a nuclear weapon in Pokhran, Rajasthan, Roy wrote an essay with the title 'The End of Imagination', which was a strong criticism of the government's nuclear policies. It was published in her collection called 'The Cost of Living', in which she also *crusaded* against India's large hydroelectric dam projects in the states of Maharashtra, Madhya Pradesh and Gujarat. She has since devoted herself solely to non-fiction and politics, publishing two more collections of essays, as well as to working for social causes.

She was in the news recently (in 2006) after she rejected the national award given by the Central Sahitya Akademi to the best Indian writer in English. Arundhati explained that although she had no quarrel with the Akademi, she was turning down the award as a protest against the policies of the government.

Unfamiliar words

activist (noun) : a person who strongly and actively supports some political or social cause

embark on : to begin something

bohemian lifestyle : living a free life, doing what you feel interested in and not following the usual customs

crusade (verb) : to fight for some cause

Comprehension questions

1. What is Arundhati Roy famous for?
2. What are Arundhati Roy's connections with Kerala?
3. Why has she been described as an 'activist'? Give examples of her activism.
4. We are told that when Arundhati Roy was in Delhi, she lived in a small hut with a tin roof and made a living by selling empty bottles. Why did she do this?

5. What kind of a person do you think Arundhati Roy is? Can you choose three words to describe her personal qualities?
6. Do you think Roy's method of protest would have any impact on the government? Why?

Vocabulary

Fill in the blanks in the sentences below, using appropriate words from the given list. (Use verbs in their correct tense forms.)

1. He has been .... for a ban on smoking and has written a number of articles in newspapers.
2. She has just completed writing a novel and plans to .... on writing another one soon.
3. She has joined a group of .... who are demanding the resignation of the chief minister.

activists, embark, bohemian, crusade

3

Read through the passage below and answer the questions that follow.

Kathakali, meaning 'story dance', combines the *emotionalism* and *tension* of drama with the grace and *visual* beauty of dance. The facial expressions and body movements of the dance bring out the emotions of each character.

Although the stories often have female characters, the dancers are always male. This is because Kathakali is a very *masculine* dance, requiring *vigorous* movement and a great deal of muscular control. The dancer never stands erect; his knees are spread out and his legs form a *rhombus*, with the hands bent at the elbow and his palms on his hips. The feet are never flat on the ground and still the actor maintains perfect balance.

A Kathakali performance traditionally begins at 8 p.m. and goes on until dawn the following morning. It is preceded at sunset by the 'Kelikottu', which is the playing of drums, gongs and cymbals, to inform local people of the night's performance. Nowadays performances are given in auditoriums, with footlights and microphones, and do not last more than three to four hours.

Kathakali plays are mainly based on the stories from the Hindu epics, the 'Mahabharata', the 'Ramayana' and the 'Bhagavata Purana'. The characters represent mythological beings—*devas* or gods and *asuras* or demons, as well as human beings. The costume and make-up transform the actor mentally and physically.

Kathakali's origin and development owe much to the royal family of Travancore. The Raja of Kottarakara (in the 17th century) was the earliest *exponent* of this art. During his time Kathakali plays were staged continuously for twenty-four hours without a break.

Unfamiliar words

emotionalism (noun) : the presence of strong emotions (feelings)

tension (noun) : the nervousness and excitement one feels in the presence of some danger

visual (adj.) : something that can be seen through the eyes

masculine (adj.) : manly; having the qualities expected in a man

vigorous (adj.) : using a lot of energy

rhombus (noun) : a shape with four equal straight sides, especially one that is not square

exponent (noun) : one who practises a particular form of some art (e.g., dance or music)

Comprehension questions

1. How does Kathakali combine dance and drama forms?
2. When and where did Kathakali begin?
3. Why are Kathakali dancers always male?
4. How are the Kathakali performances of today different from the traditional performances?

5. What is ‘Kelikottu’?
6. What kind of characters are found in a Kathakali play?

Vocabulary

Fill in the blanks in the sentences below, using appropriate words from the given list.

1. There was .... in the city after a student was arrested by the police.
2. While walking is good enough for older people, children need more .... exercise.
3. The woman surprised me by speaking in a deep, ... voice.
4. Music depends on the use of sounds, but dancing is a .... art.
5. Pandit Jasraj is an .... of Hindustani music.

vigorous, masculine, exponent, tension, visual, emotional

4

Read through the passage below and answer the questions that follow.

Amitabh Bachchan, popularly known as Big B, was born in Allahabad, Uttar Pradesh, on 11 October 1942. Amitabh is an *iconic* actor whose career in Indian cinema has *spanned* four decades. His father, Harivansh Rai Bachchan, was a well-known Hindi poet. (‘Bachchan’ was the pen-name adopted by the poet, but it has now become the family surname.) Amitabh attended Boys’ High School in Allahabad, followed by Sherwood College in Nainital and earned a degree in science from Delhi University.

His first film was ‘Saat Hindustani’ (1969). He became well known as a movie star in 1973 after the success of ‘Abhimaan’ and ‘Zanjeer’, which were followed by box office successes such as ‘Sholay’, ‘Amar Akbar Anthony’, ‘Trishul’, ‘Don’ and ‘Deewar’.

He often played the role of an angry young man fighting a corrupt establishment—a theme that had immense appeal in India at that time.

In an age when film producers had certain physical norms for the hero, Amitabh was *written off*, due to his *unconventional* looks and tall, *lanky* frame. His deep *baritone* voice, which is regarded as his biggest *asset*, once failed to get him a job as a news presenter at All India Radio. The success of 'Zanjeer' and 'Sholay' changed all that. Audiences adored his on-screen presence and *flair* for comedy.

Many of his films in the 1970s followed a set formula: a poor childhood, parents murdered or separated after birth, survival through *street-smart* ways, entry of a villain (usually a social oppresser or a smuggler or his parents' killer or a long-lost father), some comedy scenes and sad scenes, songs, dances, an action *finale* and a dying speech. Critics would regard most of these 1970s films as *run-of-the-mill* 'masala' movies with *creaking* plots and poor production values. However, Amitabh's screen presence lifted them to incredible heights of popularity.

Amitabh continued making films all through the 1980s and 1990s, but his movies were not very successful during this period. Industry gossip said that the actor's career had come to an end. But Amitabh proved his critics wrong. In 1999, in a BBC online poll, he was named 'Superstar of the Millennium'. In 2000, he was chosen to be the host for 'Kaun Banega Crorepati', a television game-show which became an enormous success. While the show was on, street traffic dropped dramatically, and restaurants and movie theatres complained of *diminishing clientèle*. Critics were forced to admit that Amitabh could still pull big crowds. The show has recently started *airing* again to similar levels of interest.

Unfamiliar words

iconic (adj.) : greatly loved and respected and having a very special position

span (verb) : to stretch across (a period of time)

to write someone off : to remove (in one's mind) someone's name from the list of those who could be selected for some job

unconventional (adj.)	: different from what is usual or expected
lanky (adj.)	: unattractively tall and thin
baritone (noun/adj.)	: a deep male voice
asset (noun)	: something that you possess, which gives you an advantage over others
flair (noun)	: a natural ability to do something
street-smart (adj.)	: qualities or skills of a person who has faced many difficulties in life and has, as a result, learnt to take care of himself/herself
finale (noun)	: the climax or highest point in a film, generally coming near the end
run-of-the-mill	: very ordinary or common, having no special qualities
'masala' movies	: 'Masala' is a Hindi word meaning 'spices'. A 'masala movie' is a film containing a lot of exciting action, songs, dances, etc., which appeal to the audience
creaking (adj.)	: A 'creaking door' is a door that makes a loud sound when it is opened, because the hinges (the movable metal parts which are used to hang the door) need oiling. If you say that a film has a 'creaking plot', it means that it has a poor and dull story.
diminishing (adj.)	: smaller and less important
clientèle (noun)	: the people who regularly visit a restaurant, cinema, etc.
air (verb)	: to show something to the public; to broadcast a television programme

Comprehension questions

1. Say whether the following statements are True (T) or False (F).
   a. Amitabh Bachchan's father was an actor.
   b. Bachchan's first film was not very successful.
   c. Film producers chose Bachchan as the hero of their films because he was the kind of hero people wanted.
   d. There was not much variety in his early films.
   e. Television has added to Bachchan's popularity.
2. What is the usual role that Amitabh Bachchan played?
3. Why did Bachchan find it difficult at first to be accepted in films?
4. Which quality is most responsible for his success as an actor?
5. What made his films so popular during the 1970s?

6. 'Amitabh proved his critics wrong.' What does this sentence mean in the passage?

Vocabulary

Fill in the blanks in the sentences below, using appropriate words from the given list.

1. The girl has a .... for music and I am sure she will become a good singer.
2. His wiriting is quite ....
3. Ajay is an .... to the organisation.
4. The doctor lost his .... after he raised his fees.
5. The old house has a wooden floor which .... when someone walks across it.

unconventional, asset, flair, diminishing, clientele, creaks

5

Read through the passage below and answer the questions that follow.

Raja Ravi Varma (1848–1906), who is sometimes described as the father of modern Indian painting, achieved recognition for his *depiction* of scenes from the Hindu epics. He was born in the royal family of Kilimanoor, which is 75 kilometres from Thiruvananthapuram. He showed talent as an artist at a very young age and received the *patronage* of the Maharaja of Travancore, who arranged for his training under the palace painter, Ramaswamy Naidu. He was later taught oil painting by the British painter, Theodor Jenson. The power and forceful expression of European painting *fascinated* Ravi Varma and his own painting shows the influence of the European painters of his time.

Ravi Varma became famous after he had won an award for an exhibition of his paintings in Vienna in 1873. He travelled throughout India in search of subjects. He is particularly noted for his paintings depicting *episodes* from the story of Dushyanta and Shakuntala, and that of Nala and Damayanti, both taken from the 'Mahabharata'. Ravi Varma's representation of mythological characters has become a part of the Indian imagination. If one has to imagine, for example, what Sita or Draupadi looked like, one would immediately think of these characters as they appear in Ravi Varma's paintings. He was—and still is—criticised for being too showy and *sentimental* in his style of painting. However his work remains very popular in India. In recent years some of his paintings have been bought by art collectors at *fabulous* prices.

Unfamiliar words

depiction (noun) : the act of showing or presenting something, through pictures or words

patronage (noun) : the help or support given, usually by a rich and powerful person, to an artist, musician, etc.

fascinate (verb) : to be of very great interest to someone

episode (noun) : one part of a long story

sentimental (adj.) : showing too much feeling

fabulous (adj.) : so great or good that it is difficult to imagine or believe

Comprehension questions

1. Say whether the following statements about Ravi Varma are True (T) or False (F).
   a. He was a prince.
   b. He was a self-taught artist.
   c. He started painting when he was a child.
   d. He is famous for his portraits of well-known people.
   e. Some people think that his work is too plain.
2. Answer the following questions.
   a. Who helped Ravi Varma to become a successful artist?
   b. What inspired Ravi Varma most in his painting?

c. What made Ravi Varma famous as an artist?
d. Which of his paintings are famous?
e. What are the qualities of his paintings that are not liked by some people?

Vocabulary

Fill in the blanks in the sentences below using appropriate words from the given list. (Use verbs in their correct tense forms.)

1. The film .... life in India a hundred years ago.
2. Her business grew very fast as she received the .... of influential persons.
3. The teacher became .... when her students gave her a birthday present.
4. I missed the last .... of the television serial.
5. The food is wonderful. In fact, it is absolutely ....

episode, fabulous, patronage, depict, sentimental

6

Read through the passage below and answer the questions that follow.

Spices are *aromatic* vegetable products derived from the roots, seeds, leaves or bark of certain plants and trees. The term 'spice' was formerly applied also to *incense* or perfume, but modern usage limits the term to *flavourings* used in food or drinks, although many spices have additional commercial uses, for example, as *ingredients* of medicines, perfumes, incense and soaps.

India has been the home of spices for more than 6000 years. Even today, it is one of the world's largest exporters of spices, the majority of which come from the state of Kerala. Spice plants need rocky soil and plenty of moisture for their growth, both of which are available in the hills of Kerala.

The earliest mention of the use of spices is found in the Vedas. The Rig Veda lists more than a thousand medicinal plants. The story of Indian spices thus goes back 7000 years.

To understand the amazing *prestige* of spices in ancient times we must remember that in those days food was not so varied or *palatable*. There were no potatoes, corn, tea, coffee or chocolate. There were no lemons with which to prepare refreshing beverages, and neither was there any sugar with which to sweeten them. However, a dash of pepper, a little cinnamon or ginger, mixed with even the *coarsest* dishes, could make them palatable.

In modern times we can use *refrigeration* to keep food fresh for months or even years, but in the ancient world refrigerators were unknown. There was no way of storing food and preventing it from going bad. Spices were therefore freely used to preserve food, as well as to hide the taste of food which was not very fresh.

The earliest trading caravans known in history carried spices. The early civilisations of the Mediterranean had a *craving* for spices from India. The Egyptians used herbs and spices in many of their daily activities as early as 2000 BC. The Romans sailed to India from Egypt in search of spices even in the first century AD. The demand for spices spread like a wave over Europe. Wars were fought over the ownership of spices. In Europe, during the Middle Ages, a pound of ginger was worth the price of a sheep; a pound of *mace* would buy three sheep or half a cow; and cloves cost the equivalent of about $20 a pound. Pepper, however, fetched the highest price. Pepper was so valuable that it was counted out corn by corn. In the 11th century, many towns kept their accounts in pepper; taxes and rents were paid in this spice; and a sack of pepper was worth a man's whole life.

Unfamiliar words

aromatic (adj.) : having an attractive smell

incense (noun) : a substance that gives out a very pleasant smell when it is burnt and that is often used during worship

flavouring (noun) : something that is added to food to improve its taste

ingredient (noun) : a substance that is used in making something else or is a part of it

prestige (noun) : honour or respect

palatable (adj.) : having a good taste

coarse (adj.) : rough; having no beauty or delicacy

refrigeration (noun) : storing food at a very low temperature so that it does not go stale

craving (noun) : a very powerful desire for something

mace (noun) : a kind of spice obtained from the fruit of a plant

Comprehension questions

1. List some of the uses of spices in the modern times.
2. What has made Kerala rich in spices?
3. What are the spices which have been mentioned in this passage? Do you know the English names of some other spices?
4. Would you call coffee a spice? Why (or why not)?
5. Why is India known as the home of spices?
6. Why were spices considered so valuable in the old days? Which was the most valuable spice?

Vocabulary

Fill in the blanks in the sentences below using appropriate words from the given list.

1. Doctors have a lot of .... in society.
2. Children often have a .... for sweets.
3. Coconut milk is an .... in many Malayali dishes.
4. The curtain material is rather ....
5. Bitter gourd becomes more .... if it is stuffed with a spicy filling and fried.

ingredient, palatable, prestige, coarse, craving

7

Read through the following passage and answer the questions that follow.

'Chemmeen' is a classic work by Thakazhi Sivasankara Pillai, one of the giants of Malayalam literature. This classic novel, set in Kerala, depicts the lives and sufferings of the fishing community with great *sensitivity*. Winner of the President's Award, 'Chemmeen' is a tragic tale with great emotional appeal. It has been translated into 14 Indian languages as well as English and a number of European languages.

The central character in the novel is Chembankunju, an *arrogant* and ambitious fisherman whose one aim in life is to own a boat and a net. Sacrificing the little joys and pleasures of life, he saves whatever he can and succeeds in buying a boat with the help of Pareekutty, a young Muslim trader, on condition that the fish caught by him will be sold to Pareekutty alone.

Chembankunju's daughter, Karuthamma, falls in love with Pareekutty. However, Karuthamma's mother, Chakki, warns her daughter that the customs of their community will not allow her to marry Pareekutty, who is an outsider.

Karuthamma gives up her love for Pareekutty and is married to Palani, an orphan youth. After the wedding, Karuthamma accompanies her husband to his village and sets up her own home. When her mother suddenly falls ill, her father asks Karuthamma to return home and look after her mother, but Karuthamma is unwilling to leave her husband's side. In anger, Chembankunju *disowns* Karuthamma.

After acquiring a boat Chembankunju becomes greedy and breaks his promise to sell his fish to Pareekutty, as the latter is unable to give him ready cash. Chembankunju's greed and dishonesty drive Pareekutty to *bankruptcy*.

Although Karuthamma is faithful to her husband Palani, the story of her love for Pareekutty spreads and *haunts* Palani. Palani's friends refuse to take him fishing with them because of the *scandal*. Karuthamma swears to her husband that she is *chaste* and Palani believes her. He decides to go fishing alone.

By a strange stroke of destiny, Karuthamma and Pareekutty meet one moonlit night. Their old love is awakened and they join in an *ecstatic* embrace when Palani is away at sea. Kadalamma, the goddess of the sea, is annoyed and punishes Karuthamma. Palani is caught in a *treacherous undercurrent*. The sea in its fury devours Palani as the lovers find bliss in each other's arms. Next morning the lovers, hand in hand, are found dead, having been washed ashore.

The story of 'Chemmeen' has many layers of meaning. At one level it tells us that true love recognises no religious or cultural boundaries. But it also shows us that passionate, uncontrolled love can destroy as well as save human beings. The novel also shows how greed and jealousy can cause people to change. While its power and *grandeur* flow from the wild and powerful ocean that rules the fishing community, its poetic beauty lies in its depiction of the small moments of joy and sorrow that can mark the lives of ordinary people.

The novel has been made into a memorable Malayalam movie, directed by Ramu Kariat.

Unfamiliar words

sensitivity (noun) : the ability to share the feelings of others

disown (verb) : to refuse to accept someone as a member of your family or group

bankruptcy (noun) : the state of having no money at all

haunt (verb) : to trouble someone for a long time or to remain in the mind for a long time (Ghosts are said to haunt people.)

scandal (noun) : widespread public outrage and loss of reputation

chaste (adj.) : of good character (generally used to describe a woman's morality)

ecstatic (adj.) : extremely happy

treacherous (adj.) : that cannot be trusted and is likely to harm you

undercurrent (noun) : a current in the sea that pulls people away from the land

grandeur (noun) : very great beauty

Comprehension questions

1. Which section of society does 'Chemmeen' depict?
2. Who, according to you, is the hero of this novel? Why do you think so?
3. What message does 'Chemmeen' have for the reader?
4. Who is Kadalamma? What part does she play in the novel?
5. Why is 'Chemmeen' considered a great novel?

Vocabulary

Fill in the blanks in the sentences below using appropriate words from the given list.

1. She was .... when she heard that her son had won the first prize.
2. The .... of the mountain had a powerful effect on my mind.
3. I nearly drowned in the sea when I was a child, and the memory .... me still.
4. How can you have a feast when so many people are starving? You should have more ....
5. I always thought of him as a friend, but he proved to be ....

treacherous, grandeur, ecstatic, scandal, sensitivity, haunts

8

Read the passage below and answer the questions that follow.

Motor vehicles run on either petrol or diesel, both of which are produced by refining petroleum, the thick, dark oil taken out from the depths of the earth. Petroleum is called a fossil fuel as it comes from fossils—the remains of animals and plants which lived on the earth millions of years ago and lie buried deep inside the earth.

The store of fossil fuels (mainly petroleum and coal) inside the earth is limited, since no more of these fuels is being produced now. Once the store is used up, we will not have any more petrol or diesel for our aeroplanes, cars, trucks and buses. Fossil fuels are therefore called non-renewable sources of energy.

As the store of fossil fuels is being used up very fast, scientists have been looking for *alternative* sources of energy. Fortunately, they have been able to produce fuel for diesel and petrol engines from plant sources. Scientists have learnt to convert the oil *extracted* from the seeds of soya beans into a liquid fuel which has been given the name 'bio-diesel'. Bio-diesel is also extracted from groundnuts, rape-seed oil and oil from a plant called jatropha. Unlike petroleum, fuel extracted from plants is a renewable source of energy. Once a plant has been harvested, another plant can grow in its place. Plants get their energy mainly from the sun, which is an unending source of energy.

It has been found that bio-diesel produces much less pollution than the fuels which are now being used in engines. It is generally mixed with diesel, in the ration 1:4, but engines can be run on pure bio-diesel.

Unfamiliar words

alternative (adj.) : something that can be used in place of something else
extract (verb) : to take something out of something else

Comprehension questions

1. What are fossil fuels? What is the name given to them and why?
2. What is bio-diesel? How is it obtained?
3. What advantage does bio-diesel offer over ordinary diesel?
4. What is the difference between renewable and non-renewable sources of energy?
5. What kind of fuel is likely to be used by motor vehicles in future?
6. What are the advantages of bio-diesel?

9

Read through the passage below and answer the questions that follow.

Malayalam is the mother tongue of 35 million Malayalis, ninety per cent of whom live in Kerala. The remainder are scattered over different parts of India and the world, including Malaysia, Singapore, the countries surrounding the Persian Gulf, Africa, Europe and North America.

Malayalis are well-known for their ability to adjust easily to their surroundings. Wherever a Malayali goes, from New Delhi to New York, he becomes a part of the local scene, though Kerala is always present in his heart.

Like its speakers, the Malayalam language also has been open to foreign influences. Malayalam literature reflects this *spirit of accommodation* and has, over the centuries, developed a tradition which, although deeply rooted in the native soil of Kerala, is truly *universal* in spirit. It is remarkably free from the prejudices that have *marred* the literature of certain other parts of our country. To its basic Dravidian stock have been added elements borrowed or adopted from non-Dravidian languages such as Sanskrit, Arabic, French, Portuguese and English. The earliest of these associations was with Tamil, which, according to many linguists, is the root language from which Malayalam was born. Sanskrit, however, accounts for the largest of the 'foreign' influences, followed closely in recent times by English. This broad-based *cosmopolitanism* has indeed become a *distinctive feature* of Malayalam language and literature.

Unfamiliar words

spirit of accommodation (noun phrase) : the willingness to accept things that have come from other lands and make them a part of yourself

universal (adj.) : belonging to the whole world and not to any particular country or place

mar (verb; past tense 'marred') : to spoil or lower the quality of something

cosmopolitanism (noun) : the quality of being open and willing to accept 'foreign' elements and not being narrow in one's outlook

distinctive feature : a quality that makes you different from others

Comprehension questions

1. How many Malayalis live outside Kerala? Choose the right answer from the options given in brackets. (a. 3.5 million b. 35 million c. 10 million)
2. What, according to the writer, is the quality that is common to Malayalis as well as to the Malayalam language?
3. What makes Malayalam literature different from the literature of some other parts of India?
4. What is the relationship between Tamil and Malayalam?
5. Which language has had the greatest influence on Malayalam?

Vocabulary

Fill in the blanks in the sentences below using appropriate words from the given list.

1. You can find people from all parts of India living together in Mumbai. It is a very .... city.
2. Music is .... Wherever you go, you will find some form of music.
3. He never speaks English because he has a .... against the language.
4. She wanted to settle in Himachal Pradesh but had to return to Tamil Nadu as she was unable to .... herself to the cold climate.
5. The hotel is full. You cannot find any .... here.

adjust, accommodation, universal, cosmopolitan, prejudice

10

Read through the passage below and answer the questions that follow.

Health tourism is an important industry in Kerala, and thousands of foreign visitors come every year to its 'vaidyashalas'. These centres of ayurvedic medicine offer *packages* of treatment that promise not only to cure diseases such as arthritis and asthma, for which there are no cures in Western medicine, but also to *reverse* the aging process and make the body young and vigorous again.

Although ayurveda has been practised in India for more than 3000 years, it seems to have become specially popular in the West during the last 25 years. This is mainly due to the feeling that the strong drugs used in Western medicine have harmful effects on the body, although they cure many kinds of diseases.

Kerala has been a major centre for ayurveda for hundreds of years. In fact, it is said that ayurveda is practised in its purest form in Kerala. Kerala's balanced climate and the abundance of forests, rich in medicinal plants and herbs, has encouraged the development of ayurveda.

The word 'ayurveda' is derived from two Sanskrit words: 'ayu' (life) and 'veda' (knowledge). Ayurveda, therefore, can be described as 'the knowledge of life'.

According to ayurveda, the body is controlled by three natural *elements*, known as 'vata', 'pitta' and 'kapha'. The body is healthy when there is a balance between these elements; but when there is an excess of any element, the body shows signs of some disease. Ayurveda treats not just the *affected* part of the body, but the individual as a whole, by removing from the body all *toxic* substances which cause disease.

Unfamiliar words

package (noun) : a number of things which are sold together to a customer

reverse (verb) : to cause something to move backwards

element (noun) : a substance which is present in many other substances but cannot be broken down into smaller chemical parts

affected (adj.) : showing the effects of some disease
toxic (adj.) : poisonous and harmful to the body

Comprehension questions

1. Define the importance of health fourism in Kerala.
2. What are the main treatments available in ayurveda?
3. Why is ayurveda so highly developed in Kerala?
4. How is ayurveda different from Western medicine?
5. What is the basic premise on which ayurveda rests?
6. How is ayurveda different in this way from the western methods of treatment?

Vocabulary

Fill in the blanks in the sentences below using appropriate words from the given list.

1. The diesel engines of trucks produce .... gases.
2. The failure of the monsoon has .... agriculture.
3. There is an .... of humour in Shakespeare's drama.
4. People are leaving the state and moving to other parts of India. It may not be possible to .... this trend.
5. The travel agents are offering a holiday .... which includes air tickets and accommodation in a three-star hotel in Goa.

reverse, affected, substance, package, toxic, element

11

Read through the passage below and answer the questions that follow.

(This is an *extract* from an interview with Mahendra Singh Dhoni, India's wicket-keeper batsman, on 12 September 2005)

Interviewer : Could you tell us something about your background and how you reached the national level in cricket?

Dhoni : Well, I grew up in Ranchi, in the state of Jharkhand, where not much cricket is played. So it was rather difficult for me to reach the national level. Actually, I started off as a footballer, but after a couple of years I shifted to cricket, while I was still in school. I managed to get into the under-16 state team and then the under-19 team. I made my *debut* in the Ranji Trophy tournament in 1999–2000. My performance in domestic tournaments was quite *consistent*. Then, last year, I was selected for the India-A team that toured Kenya and Zimbabwe, and that was the turning point for me. I played well on that tour and later got into the Indian team on the tour of Bangladesh.

Interviewer : You are one of the hardest hitters of the ball in the game. What is the secret of 'Dhoni Power'?

Dhoni : I don't know if there is any secret. I seldom go to a *gym* for *workouts*. But maybe the training I received as a footballer has helped.

Interviewer : What about the story of the 4 litres of milk that you are said to drink everyday?

Dhoni (laughing) : I'm afraid that's a bit of an *exaggeration*. But yes, I do love milk and drink about a litre a day. Earlier, it used to be just plain milk, but now it's mostly milk with hot chocolate.

Interviewer : Not only do you hit those big sixes, but you are also an excellent runner between the wickets, in spite of the conditions being hot and humid. So are you a *fitness freak*?

Dhoni : Not really. I think it just comes naturally to me. You know, my family is from Almora, from the mountains of Uttaranchal. One has to be very fit to live there. I suppose physical fitness must be in my *genes*, although I have never actually lived in the mountains. But I am working hard on my fitness right now, following the training schedule given by Gregory King, our trainer.

Interviewer : What aspects of your game do you want to improve?

Dhoni : My batting as well as my wicket keeping. I would love to improve my wicket keeping, especially against the spinners. We have quality spinners in our team like Harbhajan and Anil Kumble, and it's really difficult to keep wickets when they are bowling. So that's one thing I must improve. And, of course, my batting. I have been shifted quite a lot in the batting order, from batting at number 6 or 7 to batting at number 3, or even opening the innings. So the more I play, the more I must get used to different batting *slots*. Lots of things are going on in my head . . .

Interviewer : How do you spend your day when you are not playing in matches?

Dhoni : Oh, I listen to a lot of music. I love music, you know. Then, I love motorbikes; I enjoy riding my motorbike. And I like playing computer games. I play a bit of badminton when I get time. But I love bikes more than anything else.

Unfamiliar words

extract (noun) : a short piece taken from a speech or piece of writing

début (noun) : the first public appearance of someone

consistent (adj.) : maintaining the same standard or quality over a period of time

gym (noun) : short form of 'gymnasium', a place where one goes for exercise

workout (noun) : physical exercise taken to increase one's fitness and strength

exaggeration (noun) : something which is not entirely true, but is said to make something appear better or bigger than it really is

fitness freak (noun phrase) : a person who takes a lot of exercise to maintain his/her fitness (good health)

genes (noun) : chemicals present in the cells of the body which pass on some of the qualities of the parent (father or mother) to the child

slot (noun) : a particular place or position which a person/event occupies

Comprehension questions

1. Why was it difficult for Dhoni to find a place in the Indian cricket team?
2. When was he first selected for a national team?
3. What makes Dhoni special as a cricketer?
4. What, according to Dhoni himself, is the secret of his physical fitness?
5. Why does Dhoni think it is necessary for him to improve his wicket-keeping?
6. What does Dhoni have to say about his batting?
7. What is Dhoni's favourite way of relaxing?

Vocabulary

Fill in the blanks in the sentences below using appropriate words from the given list.

1. My daughter is learning Bharatanatyam and will make her .... on the stage next month.
2. It is an .... to say that there was a huge crowd at the meeting. Actually, there were no more than a hundred people there.
3. Pathan has scored centuries in the last three matches. His performance has been very ....
4. I am going to read out an .... from the speech which the president gave on Republic Day.

5. The doctor is very busy today, but he is free between 3.00 and 3.30 p.m. You can see him during this ....

exaggeration, entry, consistent, debut, slot, extract

12

Read through the passage below and answer the questions that follow.

In 1951, a white tiger cub was captured in the forests of Rewa State, in Rajasthan. Before this, no one had reported the existence of white tigers, but today, they can be seen in many zoos around the world and they attract a lot of visitors, specially children, because of their unusual appearance. Many people think that the white tiger belongs to a different *species* from the ordinary Bengal tiger, which has a bright orange-coloured coat with black stripes, but in fact they belong to the same species. Sometimes, a pair of ordinary tigers will produce white cubs. This is a very rare event and happens only once in approximately 10,000 births. The white colour of the offspring is due to some changes in the genes of the parents.

White tigers have pink noses and white or cream-colored fur with black, grey or chocolate-colored stripes. Their eyes are usually blue, but may be green or *amber*. There are around 600 white tigers in the world.

White tigers have always been extremely rare in the wild and have only been spotted in India. The reason why they are so rare is that the white colour makes for poor *camouflage* when the tiger is hunting or hiding.

Unfamiliar words

species (noun) : a family of animals and plants which have many common physical qualities

amber (adj.) : having a yellowish-orange colour

camouflage (noun) : A natural system of protection which some plants and animals have, due to their colouring which is similar to that of the surrounding trees, rocks, etc., and because of which they cannot be easily seen.

Comprehension questions

1. Which was the first reported instance of a white tiger?
2. Describe the white tiger in detail. How are white tigers different in appearance from ordinary tigers?
3. How can we explain the fact that some tigers are white?
4. Why are white tigers so rare?
5. In which parts of the world are white tigers found?

13

Read through the passage below and answer the questions that follow.

The Periyar *tiger reserve*, situated in the Idukki district of Kerala, among the Western Ghats, is one of nature's many gifts to the state. It takes its name from the Periyar river, which flows through the forest. A dam was built across the river in 1895, creating the artificial Periyar lake in the heart of the forest, which makes it specially attractive to animals as well as the visitors who come to see them.

At that time, a large part of the modern state of Kerala formed the kingdom of Travancore. The Maharaja was an *enlightened* ruler who understood the importance of *natural conservation*. It was the Maharaja of Travancore who, in 1934, turned the forests around the lake into a *game sanctuary*, where no hunting of animals was allowed.

Periyar was declared a tiger reserve in 1978, under the Project Tiger scheme launched by the government of India to protect the Indian tiger, which was fast dying out.

Noted for its *scenic* beauty and the richness of *wildlife*, the Periyar tiger reserve attracts nature lovers from all over the world. This is the only game sanctuary in India where elephants can be observed and photographed at close quarters, while they bathe and play in the waters of the lake, from the safety of a boat.

The Periyar reserve shelters a large variety of wildlife. Among the animals frequently sighted here are the tiger, the panther, the elephant, the wild buffalo and the wild dog. There are several kinds of poisonous and non-poisonous snakes including the king cobra. Tortoises may often be seen *basking* on rocks and tree trunks by the lake. Effective measures have been taken to protect wildlife by *eliminating poaching* and the grazing of cattle.

The entry point to the Periyar reserve is Thekkadi, which is *accessible* by road from Madurai, Thiruvananthapuram and Kochi. The nearest *railhead* is Kottayam. The ideal time to visit the reserve is from October to May.

Unfamiliar words

tiger reserve (noun phrase) : a forest in which tigers live and are specially protected by the government

enlightened (adj.) : wise, with great knowledge

natural conservation (noun phrase) : the protection given to animals and plants which are in danger of dying out, mainly due to the increase in the human population

game sanctuary (noun phrase) : a forest in which hunting is not allowed, so that animals are protected. ('Game' means 'wild animals' while a 'sanctuary' is a place where one is protected and safe.)

scenic (adj.) : having natural beauty (e.g., lakes, mountains, etc.)

wildlife (noun) : plants and animals found in forests

bask (verb) : to lie or sit in the sun, enjoying its warmth

eliminate (verb) : to remove or destroy completely

poaching (noun) : the illegal killing of protected animals

accessible (adj.) : which can be easily reached

railhead (noun) : the last point which is connected by railway (after which no trains run)

Comprehension questions

1. Who created the Periyar tiger reserve? What was the idea behind the person's doing so?
2. How did the game sanctuary get its name?
3. What makes this forest different from other forests?
4. In the light of this passage, can you say why 'natural conservation' is important?
5. The Periyar reserve has been described as one of nature's gifts to Kerala. Do you agree with this description? Why?

Vocabulary

Fill in the blanks in the sentences below using appropriate words from the given list. (Use the verbs in their correct forms.)

1. During the monsoon, the roads leading to my village are flooded, and then it is not .... at all.
2. You will find many foreign tourists .... in the sun on the Kovalam beach.
3. The backwaters near Kochi are very ....
4. There are no mosquitoes here. They have been ....
5. All the children in our village are sent to school as the people are quite ....

scenic, bask, enlightened, accessible, eliminate

14

Read through the passage below and answer the questions that follow.

The *Union Territory* of Lakshadweep, earlier known as the Laccadives, is an archipelago or chain of islands in the Arabian

Sea, spreading over an area of 32 sq. km and consisting of 10 *inhabited* and 17 uninhabited islands. According to the 2001 census, Lakshadweep has a population of 60,253. Bitra, the smallest island, has a population of only 225. The island of Bangaram, previously uninhabited, has a population of 61 according to the 2001 census.

Lakshadweep is located between 8° and 12° north latitude and 71° and 74° east longitude and lies 220 to 440 km away from the coastal city of Kochi in Kerala.

Malayalam is spoken on all the islands except Minicoy, where the people speak a language known as Mahl. The entire population of Lakshadweep has been classified as scheduled tribes because of their economic and social backwardness. Ninety-three per cent of the population is Muslim. The main occupations of the people are fishing, coconut cultivation and *coir twisting*. Tourism is an *emerging* industry.

The early history of Lakshadweep is largely unknown. According to local tradition, people from the mainland first settled on these islands during the time of Cheraman Perumal, the last king of Kerala, who was converted to Islam by some Arab merchants, probably in the 9th century AD.

For several centuries, Lakshadweep was ruled by the kings of Cannanore (now Kannur). In the year 1783, the administration of the islands was taken over by Tipu Sultan, at the request of some of the islanders. After the battle of Seringapatam in 1799, when Tipu was defeated by the British, the islands were *annexed* by the East India Company and were administered from Mangalore.

Lakshadweep was made a union territory in 1956 and its name was changed from Laccadives to Lakshadweep in 1973.

Unfamiliar words

union territory (noun phrase) : a part of India that is directly controlled by the central government and does not form a part of any state

inhabited (adj.) : having people living on it (opposite: uninhabited)

coir twisting (noun) : making ropes out of coir (the thick fibre that covers coconut fruits)

emerging (adj.) : growing

annex (verb) : to occupy a place and make it a part of your own kingdom

Comprehension questions

1. Where is Lakshadweep? What was its name earlier? When did it get its new name?
2. How many islands are there in Lakshadweep? What is special about the islands of Bitra and Bangaram?
3. What is the religion of the people of Lakshadweep? What languages do they speak? What are their chief occupations?
4. When did people from the mainland first settle in Lakshadweep?
5. When did the British take over the administration of Lakshadweep and why?

15

Read through the passage below and answer the questions that follow.

William H. Gates is the co-founder and chairman of Microsoft Corporation, the world leader in software services and solutions, which helps individuals as well as business companies to achieve their full *potential.* Microsoft had revenues of US $ 36.84 billion in the *fiscal year* ending June 2004, and employs more than 55,000 people in 85 countries.

Born on 28 October 1955, Gates grew up in Seattle, in the state of Washington, with his two sisters. Their father, William H. Gates II, is a Seattle *attorney.* Their late mother, Mary Gates, was a school teacher.

Gates attended a public elementary school and the private Lakeside School. There he discovered his interest in software and began programming computers at the age of 13.

In 1973, Gates entered Harvard University, and while there he developed a version of the programming language known as BASIC, which was used for the first *microcomputer*—the MITS Altair.

In his junior year, Gates left Harvard to devote his energies to Microsoft, a company he had begun in 1975 with his childhood friend Paul Allen. Guided by the belief that the computer would become a valuable tool for every office and home, they began developing software for personal computers. Gates's *foresight* and his vision for personal computing have been central to the success of Microsoft and the software industry.

Under Gates's leadership, Microsoft's *mission* has been to continually advance and improve software technology and to make it easier, more *cost-effective* and more enjoyable for people to use computers. The company is committed to a long-term view, reflected in its investment of approximately $6.2 billion on research and development in the 2005 fiscal year.

Unfamiliar words

potential (noun) : the good qualities or the abilities which lie hidden inside a person until they are given a chance to come out into the open

fiscal year : (financial year) a period of 12 months which is used to calculate the amount of money that an individual or company has earned (In India, the financial year runs from April to March.)

attorney : lawyer (in American English)

microcomputer : a computer of small size which can be used at home or in the office (also, personal computer)

foresight (noun) : the ability to look ahead and form an idea of what is likely to happen in the future

mission (noun) : the aim or goal that one wants to achieve

cost-effective (adj.): able to produce good results without spending a lot of money

Comprehension questions

1. What is the name of the company that Bill Gates founded? When was it founded?
2. What kind of business is Microsoft engaged in? Why is it so famous?
3. Why did Bill Gates not complete his university education?

4. What was Bill Gates's earliest achievement in the world of computing?
5. How has Bill Gates guided the future of Microsoft Corporation? What are the results of his guidance?

16

Read through the passage below and answer the questions that follow.

Mammootty, the *megastar* of Malayalam cinema, whose real name is Mohammad Kutty, was born on 7 September 1953. Regarded by many as one of the most talented actors of Indian cinema, he *captivates* the audience with his deep voice and talent.

Although he is a lawyer by training, Mammootty always wanted to be an actor. He first appeared in the Malayalam film 'Devalokam', which, unfortunately, was never released. His talent was first noticed in the movie 'Vilkanundu Swapnangal' (1980). He was groomed by the director K. G. George, who gave him a number of different roles in films such as 'Valarthumrigangal', 'Yavanika' and 'Aadaminte Vaariyellu'. His *firebrand* performances in these films saw the birth of a new superstar.

He was supported by good directors and scriptwriters such as Adoor Gopalakrishnan and M. T. Vasudevan Nair. His controlled acting never crossed limits, and the presentation of M. T. Vasudevan Nair's hard-hitting dialogues made Mammootty the *heart-throb* of Malayalam film viewers.

Mammotty has seen many ups and downs in his long career, but each time he is down, he has made a comeback to win people's hearts. His career saw a *spectacular* rise after the release of director Joshi's 'New Delhi'. It *heralded* the rebirth of Mammootty the super star.

Mammootty touched new heights in the film 'Oru Vadakkan Veeragatha', an M. T. Vasudevan Nair creation, which brought him the national award for the best actor. The *breathtaking* portrayal of Basheer in Adoor Gopalakrishnan's art movie 'Mathilukal' won him the national award for best acting once more while his superb acting in T. V. Chandran's 'Ponthan Mada', another art film, won him the national award for a third time.

Mammootty is equally popular in Tamil, Telugu, and Hindi films. Even at the age of 53, he is one of the busiest actors in Malayalam cinema.

Unfamiliar words

mega-star (noun) : someone who is at the highest level of success and popularity

captivate (verb) : to win someone's complete love and respect

firebrand (adj./noun) : dynamic; full of energy

heart-throb (noun) : someone who is greatly loved by everyone

spectacular (adj.) : exciting; attracting everyone's attention

herald (verb) : to announce or bring about something new

breathtaking (adj.) : exciting

Comprehension questions

1. What was Mammootty's training and background?
2. Would it be reasonable to call him 'one of the most talented actors of Indian cinema'? What evidence is there to support this view?
3. What was one advantage that Mammootty had with regard to his career?
4. 'Mammootty has seen many ups and down in his career, but each time he is down he has made a comeback.' What is the amazing quality of Mammootty that is brought out in this sentence?
5. Do you know of any other famous person who has seen many ups and downs, and has been able to make a comeback after 'being down'?

17

Read through the passage below and answer the questions that follow.

The Jews are a race whose original home was in Israel. The Jewish religion is one of the oldest in the world. However, the Jews were forced to leave their homeland about 2000 years ago and were scattered in different parts of the world. Now their country, Israel, has been returned to them and they have a home again.

One group of Jews came to India many hundreds of years ago and made Kerala their home. The 'Cochini Jews' as they are called live in the city of Cochin, or Kochi and form the oldest and largest community of Jews in India.

It is not clear when the first Cochini Jews arrived or where they came from. They were not part of a single *migration,* but settled in the area around Kochi at different times. According to one legend, the forefathers of the Cochini Jews came to India during the time of King Solomon, the famous king of the Jews whose name is found in the Bible, more than 3000 years ago. King Solomon is said to have had trade relations with a southern kingdom, which was most probably the present state of Kerala. Later on, a second migration of Jews from Spain took place about 1000 years ago. The Spanish Jews also settled near Kochi, but they lived separately from the Indian Jews and did not mix with them.

The people of Kerala take pride in the fact that their land was famous all over the world as long ago as 3000 BC, and merchants from many lands, including the Romans, Greeks, Arabs, and Chinese, have been visiting Kerala since the times of King Solomon. They were drawn to Kerala mainly by the rich spice and textile trades. Among these visitors were many Jewish merchants, many of whom settled in Kerala. The existence of the Jewish community in South India was known to other Jews outside India. These Jewish merchants were very influential and were mainly responsible for the early prosperity of Kerala. In gratitude for their contribution to the kingdom, the ruler, Sri Parkaran Iravi Vanmar, gave the village of Anjuvannam to the head of the Jewish community and pronounced him the prince of this village. These Jewish rulers were given all the rights reserved for ruling families in India.

There is no agreement among scholars about the exact date when this 'Jewish kingdom' was established. Some claim it was in the 4th century AD while others believe it happened at a much later date—around the 10th century. According to the

Cochini Jews themselves, the princely rights were given to them in 379 AD.

Today there are only about 70 Jews in Kochi, although the number was about 3000 in the 1940s.

Unfamiliar words

migration (noun) : the act of moving from one country or place and settling down in some other place

Comprehension questions

1. Who are the 'Cochini Jews'? When and why did they come to India?
2. What is the relevance of King Solomon in this passage?
3. What was the contribution of Jewish merchants to the economy of Kerala?
4. When and how was the 'Jewish kingdom' set up in Kerala?
5. What was the significance of Kerala in the history of the ancient world?
6. What is the point of disagreement among scholars regarding the Jewish kingdom in India?

18

Read through the passage below and answer the questions that follow.

The 11 September 2001 attacks (frequently referred to as 9/11) were a series of *coordinated suicide attacks* upon the United States of America carried out on Tuesday, 11 September 2001, in which *hijackers* took control of four US domestic commercial airliners. The hijackers crashed two planes into the World Trade Center in Manhattan, New York City — one into each of the two tallest towers, about 18 minutes apart. Within two hours, both towers had collapsed. The hijackers crashed the third aircraft into the US Department of Defense headquarters, the Pentagon, in Arlington County, Virginia. The fourth plane crashed into a rural field in Somerset County,

Pennsylvania, 80 miles (129 km) east of Pittsburgh, following passenger resistance. The official count records 2,986 deaths in the attacks, including the hijackers.

The nineteen hijackers who carried out the attack were terrorists belonging to the Islamic Al-Qaeda organisation. The report named Osama bin Laden, a Saudi national, as the leader of Al-Qaeda and the person ultimately suspected of being responsible for the attacks, although the actual planning was undertaken by Khalid Shaikh Mohammed. Initially, Bin Laden *categorically* denied his involvement in two statements made in 2001, but admitted in a taped statement a direct link with the attacks.

The hijackers turned the planes into the largest suicide bombs in history. The 11 September 2001 attacks are among the most significant events to have occurred so far in the 20th century, in terms of its profound economic, social, political, cultural, psychological and military effects.

Unfamiliar words

coordinate (verb) : to plan and manage a number of activities happening at the same time

suicide attack (noun phrase) : an attack (usually carried out by a terrorist) in which the attacker knows he/she is sure to be killed

hijacker (noun) : a person who takes control of a plane or other vehicle by force and threatens to kill the passengers, often for political reasons

categorically (adv.) : in very clear terms, leaving no doubt

Comprehension questions

1. What is '9/11'? Why do we call it by that name?
2. What was the *modus operandi* of the hijackers?
3. Who was blamed for this incident? What was the identity of the hijackers and who claimed responsibility later for the attacks?
4. Why was '9/11' a complete success?
5. What is the global significance of this incident?

19

Read through the passage below and answer the questions that follow.

The people of Kerala have always been devoted to sports and other forms of physical activity. Some of India's greatest athletes, such as Suresh Babu, T. C. Yohannan, Valsamma, P. T. Usha and Anju George belong to Kerala.

Many traditional sports which were once popular in the villages of Kerala have almost disappeared in the last decade. Games such as Kilithattukali, Kallukali, Kallanum Policeum and Thalappandukali *evoke nostalgic* memories today. While Kilithattukali gave ample exercise to the body, Kuttiyum Kolum Kali was our own version of cricket. Many other traditional games are fast disappearing. It is a pity that the new generation of children will never have a chance to witness or enjoy these games.

However, one traditional sport which is witnessing a revival is Kalarippayattu, the martial art of Kerala. Physical fitness and great mental concentration are essential for success in this sport, which is part of Kerala's history. In the old days, only members of the Nair community, which formed Kerala's warrior class, had the right to engage in Kalarippayattu. It was used as a form of military training for the private armies maintained by local kings and chieftains, who were continually fighting among themselves. But when Kerala came under British rule, the *feuds* between local chieftains were brought under control and the Kalaris (centres of Kalarippayattu training) were closed. However, Kalarippayattu is performed with great enthusiasm at certain centres even today. This martial art is not quite dead, though its importance has been greatly reduced.

In recent times, the arrival of a number of great women athletes *ushered* in the golden age of athletics in Kerala. The first woman athlete from Kerala to make a mark in international sports was Angel Mary, who won silver medals in the pentathlon and long jump events at the 1978 Asian Games in Bangkok. The *legendary*

P. T. Usha, from the village of Payyoli, made her début at the Moscow Olympics of 1980. At the 1982 Delhi Asiad, the *trinity* of Usha, Shiny Abraham and Valsamma *dominated* women's athletics. Since then, there has been a steady flow of medals to Kerala. If it was Valsamma in 1982, it was the turn of Usha in 1984. She was expected to win a medal at the 1984 Olympic Games, but she lost a medal *by a whisker*—by only one hundredth of a second—in the 400 metres. That the 'Payyoli Express' (as Usha is referred to) is still running is a wonder for every sports lover. She was the first Malayali athlete to have reached the final of an Olympic event. However, before Usha, Shiny Abraham had reached the semi-final stage in the 800 metres in the Olympics. The next few years belonged to Usha and Shiny as they won innumerable national and international athletic events. In 2003, Anju Bobby George brought home a bronze medal from the World Athletic Championships held at Paris, reviving the hope that India may soon produce a medal winner at the Olympic Games.

Unfamiliar words

evoke (verb) : to bring an emotion (feeling) into someone's mind

nostalgic (adj.) : bringing happy memories of the past

feud (noun) : a quarrel or fight between two or more groups of people which goes on for a long time

usher in (verb) : to bring something into existence for the first time

legendary (adj.) : very famous

trinity (noun) : a group of three people

dominate (verb) : to play the most important part in something

by a whisker (adv. phrase) : by a very narrow margin

Comprehension questions

1. Say whether the following statements are True (T) or False (F).
   a. Sports have always been popular in Kerala.
   b. Kerala has produced many famous athletes and sportspersons.
   c. The traditional sports of Kerala attract a lot of people even today.

d. Kalarippayattu was practised by many people in the old days.
e. P. T. Usha is one of the most successful women athletes from Kerala.

2. Who is the 'Payyoli Express'? Why was this name given to the person?
3. Was Kalarippayattu encouraged by the British? Why? (or why not?)
4. Which period is referred to as 'the golden age of athletics'?
5. How have athletics and sports been revived in Kerala? Who are the chief contributors to this development?

20

Read through the passage below and answer the questions that follow.

The Indian Ocean earthquake of 2004, also known as the Sumatra–Andaman earthquake, was an undersea earthquake that occurred on the morning of 26 December 2004. It had a magnitude of 9.15 on the *Richter scale*, which makes it one of the most powerful earthquakes ever recorded. The only known earthquake of comparable magnitude was the Great Earthquake of Chile (magnitude 9.5), in 1960.

The Indian Ocean earthquake killed more than 283,100 people, making it one of the deadliest disasters in modern history. It lasted close to ten minutes, when most major earthquakes last no more than a few seconds. It caused the entire planet to move off its course by at least a few centimetres and triggered earthquakes elsewhere, as far away as Alaska.

The earthquake had its *epicentre* in Aceh, the northern tip of the Indonesian island of Sumatra. Aceh was *devastated*, but major damage was also suffered by Thailand and the Andaman–Nicobar islands, and to a lesser extent, Sri Lanka and India. Deaths were reported as far away as the east coast of Africa, more than 8,000 km away.

The earthquake caused the seabed to rise by several metres, displacing an estimated 30 cubic kilometres of water and triggering a huge wave, called a tsunami, that struck the coasts of several countries in the Indian Ocean. The waves, which reached a maximum height of 30 metres (100 feet), spread outwards along a length of 1200 km, reaching as far as Mexico, Chile and the Arctic. The raising of the sea bed produced a permanent rise in the global sea level by an estimated 0.1 mm.

The tsunami, like all others, behaves very differently in deep water and in shallow water. In deep ocean water, the tsunami waves form only a small hump, barely noticeable and harmless. It generally travels at a very high speed of 500 to 1000 km/h (310 to 620 mph). In shallow water near coastlines, a tsunami slows down to only tens of kilometres an hour but in doing so forms large destructive waves. Scientists investigating the damage in Aceh found evidence that the wave reached a height of 24 m (80 ft) when coming ashore along large stretches of the coastline, rising to 30 m (100 ft) in some areas when travelling inland.

The people who suffered most from this natural *calamity* are some of the poorest people on earth. Thousands have been killed, but many more have been made homeless. It will take them many years to recover, but in the meantime, we hope that those who are more fortunate will come to the aid of their suffering fellow human beings.

Unfamiliar words

Richter scale : a scale used to measure the force of an earthquake

epicentre (noun) : the place where an earthquake begins and from which it spreads to other places

devastate (verb) : to cause very great destruction

calamity (noun) : a great misfortune (a piece of bad luck)

Comprehension questions

1. Say whether the following statements are True (T) or False (F).
   a. The Indian Ocean earthquake of 2004 was the most powerful earthquake ever recorded.
   b. The earthquake lasted for a few seconds only.

   c. The earthquake caused greatest damage to Indonesia.
   d. The speed of a *tsunami* increases as it comes close to the land.
   e. The *tsunami* in 2004 was caused by a rise in the sea level.
2. What permanent effects did the earthquake produce?
3. What is a *tsunami* and how is it caused? What was the geographical extent of the damage caused by this earthquake?
4. What were some of the damages caused by the *tsunami*?
5. What is the purpose of the writer in writing this piece?

4 Written Communication

Paragraph Writing

A sentence expresses a complete thought or idea. We do not, however, always speak or write isolated sentences. In performing some of the language functions such as describing, narrating, arguing/reasoning and discussing, we need to combine a set of sentences into a larger piece of text, known as a paragraph. Paragraph writing is linked very closely to another basic skill—that of organising our thoughts on a subject, connecting them and expressing ourselves clearly. (This is an important skill that you will have to use all the time, first as students and later on in your professional lives, in writing and speaking to state facts, to examine and analyse situations and to express your opinions.) It is important, therefore, to learn and practise how to write short, coherent paragraphs.

A paragraph is a small set of sentences related to a topic or theme (or a single aspect of a much larger theme) arranged carefully in order to describe, narrate, discuss or present an argument. The best paragraphs ('best' in terms of the ease with which they can be understood) are never very long, except in scholarly or technical texts. This is because it is easy for a reader or listener to understand what is said when the information is presented in short coherent bits.

For an example that will help you understand the process of paragraph writing, look at the sentences given below.

- In some places the temperature will rise higher than two to four degrees Celsius.
- The rise in the earth's average temperature may not sound like much, but scientists are very concerned about it.
- The earth is getting warmer.

- **Some governments are encouraging wind and solar energy production.**
- The average temperature of the earth's atmosphere has been increasing by just over 0.1 degrees Celsius every ten years.
- Scientists predict that the average world temperature will rise by two to four degrees Celsius in less than a hundred years.

Note that all the sentences—except for the highlighted sentence about wind and solar energy production—deal with five pieces of information that are related to a central idea or theme, which happens to be global warming. Hence, the five sentences can be put together to form a paragraph on the topic.

Every paragraph should have a similar unity of theme, which means that it should be built around a single idea. The sentence expressing the central idea of a paragraph is called a *topic sentence*. The topic sentence is always the most general statement in the paragraph and it includes in its scope all the other specific statements made about it. It can be placed at the beginning or at the end of the paragraph, although in texts relating to science and technology, the first position is usually preferred. Sometimes the topic sentence is placed within the paragraph, but this is not very commonly done. The topic sentence in the set of sentences given above is 'The earth is getting warmer.' Now see how we can omit the highlighted sentence, that does not reinforce or contribute to the central theme in any way, and order the remaining sentences (starting with the topic sentence) in the set to form a paragraph.

> The earth is getting warmer. The average temperature of the earth's atmosphere has been increasing by just over 0.1 degrees Celsius every ten years. The rise in the earth's average temperature may not sound like much, but scientists are very concerned about it. Scientists predict that the average world temperature will rise by two to four degrees Celsius in less than a hundred years. In some places the temperature will rise higher than two to four degrees Celsius.

Note that although we have omitted the sentence not directly related to the rise in the earth's temperature, and have arranged the five relevant sentences in some kind of logical order with the topic sentence at the beginning, we do not still have an entirely coherent paragraph that could be used to convey the information on global warming. In order to have a well-connected piece of text, in which there is a clearly logical progression of thought, we will additionally have to link the individual points or ideas so that the earlier ones lead naturally to those that come later. This can be achieved by (a) using pronouns and other reference words to refer back to what appeared earlier in the paragraph, and (b) by linking the individual sentences with a special group of words called linkers, or connectives. Some commonly used connectives are listed below.

thus	however	therefore
consequently	subsequently	also
firstly	secondly	finally
on the other hand	in addition	to sum up

Sometimes we may even need to recast a sentence to make it fit better into the paragraph. See how we can use some of these techniques to improve upon the sample paragraph on global warming and give it the quality of coherence. The italicised words indicate the changes that are made to achieve coherence in the paragraph.

> The earth is getting warmer. The average temperature of *its* atmosphere has been increasing by just over 0.1 degrees Celsius every ten years. *This rise* may not sound like much, but scientists are very concerned about it. *They* predict that the average world temperature will rise by two to four degrees Celsius in less than a hundred years. *In fact*, in some places the rise will be even higher.

Some paragraphs do not have a sentence that can be identified clearly as the topic sentence. Despite this, such paragraphs too would have a central theme that is implicit and clear enough to anyone who reads them. For an example, look at the sentences below and follow the steps taken to transform them into a paragraph. We will begin by identifying a central theme that the sentences relate to and then omit the sentence(s) unrelated to the theme, order the sentences and, finally, make them more coherent by using connectives and reference words.

- Fungi are widespread.
- **There are more than 3,500 known species of bacteria.**
- Most of the infections fungi cause in humans are mild and easily treated.
- Fungi are among the four types of micro-organisms that cause diseases in humans.
- Fungi are plants that feed off other organisms, living or dead.
- It has not been a high priority to develop vaccines against fungi.

All the sentences above, except for the highlighted one, are about fungi, which is, thus, the central theme. None of the sentences, however, can be identified as the topic sentence, which states the theme explicitly. Having seen that the set does not have a topic sentence, we can order the sentences so that there is a logical progression of thought. One way of doing this is, as shown below, to start the paragraph with a statement identifying fungi in a general kind of a way—they are one of the four types of micro-organisms causing diseases in humans. The second sentence gives a clearer definition of fungi as plants that feed off other organisms. The third sentence talks about where they are found. The fourth sentence tells us that the harm they do is not very serious. The last sentence explains that for the reason stated in the previous one, high priority has not been given to developing vaccines as protection against them.

- Fungi are among the four types of micro-organisms that cause diseases in humans.
- Fungi are plants that feed off other organisms, living or dead.
- Fungi are widespread.
- Most of the infections fungi cause in humans are mild and easily treated.

– It has not been a high priority to develop vaccines against fungi.

Having ordered the jumbled sentences, we can now use connectives and reference words as well as the other techniques mentioned above to arrive at a coherent short piece of writing.

> Fungi are among the four types of micro-organisms that cause diseases in humans. *They* are plants that feed off other organisms, living or dead. Fungi are widespread. *However*, most of the infections these micro-organisms cause in humans are mild and easily treated. *Consequently*, it has not been a high priority to develop vaccines against fungi.

The following bulleted points will not only recapitulate all that was said above but also make it easy for you to follow the actual steps involved in composing short paragraphs that you may need to either write or speak about someone or something.

- Think about the topic on which you have to compose a paragraph. Good paragraphs are always based on carefully gathered facts on a topic and on the writer's opinions on it.
- Put down five to ten ideas on the topic that come to your mind.
- Go over the points to check if there are some that are irrelevant to the topic. Drop such points if you find any.
- Arrange the points in a chronological, sequential or logical order, placing the topic sentence at the beginning or the end of the paragraph. (These positions suit all kinds of themes, and are hence recommended, especially until you master the skill of composing paragraphs.)
- Use connectives, pronouns and other reference words and recast some of the sentences if you think it would make your paragraph more coherent and effective.
- Use variety in sentence length and structure to make the paragraph more interesting.
- Read the paragraph again, revise and make corrections if needed.

Remember that the best paragraphs are written in your own words, chosen carefully to express your observations, feelings and opinions. Paragraphs on personal topics need to be based on actual experiences or be purely imaginary, while paragraphs on general topics call for an awareness of current affairs and the world we live in. When asked to compose a paragraph on a general topic, it is a good idea to refer to some books to collect facts.

Fifteen short paragraphs each on personal and general topics are given below for your reference. The lengths of the paragraphs vary from five to ten sentences. In each of them, identify the topic sentence, where present, and also the connectives and reference words that make the paragraph coherent. Study the sample paragraphs carefully and note how their central themes have been developed meaningfully using supporting details and illustrations.

Sample paragraphs on personal topics

1. My views on college life

I think that life in college is far more interesting and exciting than it used to be at school. First of all, college students are treated as adults, capable of taking independent decisions about their lives and careers. We are also allowed the freedom to express our personal views on topical issues and on matters that concern us. Another reason why college life is great is that the teachers are more open and accessible, and they interact with the students more freely than our teachers did at school. Further, college students get the opportunity to read widely and to listen to learned academics and well-known personalities from different fields. Additionally, college also offers many extracurricular activities, such as debates and music competitions, for those who would like to participate in them. But above all, college life is fun because it includes picnics and longer trips with classmates and teachers.

2. The kind of books I enjoy reading

I enjoy reading fiction most of all. This includes novels as well as short stories. I especially love romances and thrillers and can spend long hours by myself if I have enough of them to read. Science fiction, however, does not really interest me because I find the stories and characters rather dull. Among non-fiction, I enjoy reading travelogues and biographies of explorers, sportspersons and artists as well as accounts of real-life adventures. Of course, there are always the newspapers and magazines that I read regularly to keep myself informed and, sometimes, to pass the time when I am free and when I cannot find a new book to read.

3. My philosophy of life

I believe that each of us must treat other people the way we would like them to treat us. We must realise that what causes pain to us will surely do the same to others as well, to a lesser or a greater degree. In fact, one of the main reasons behind all the violence and misery we find in the world today is, in my opinion, the complete lack of understanding of this basic truth. For example, none of us will be able to bear the agony of seeing our friends and the members of our family being killed, of our land and possessions being snatched away or of being humiliated, discriminated against and treated unjustly. Once we are sensitive to this fact, we will never allow ourselves to be cruel to others, whether they are human beings or animals.

4. What friendship means to me

Friendship, according to me, is one of the most wonderful things life has to offer. Friends are people who together with families fill our days with happiness and a sense of being wanted. I think that friendship is possible only when there is complete understanding and acceptance among those involved in the relationship. In addition to these qualities, a true friend is loyal and caring at all times. Further, friendship sometimes makes it necessary for us to act selflessly and make small sacrifices that would help our friends in some way. In spite of the discomfort we may experience in such situations, we feel delighted when we find that we have been able to bring peace and happiness to a person who will always have a very special place in our lives.

5. A typical working day

I am usually up at five in the morning on week days. I spend the first hour studying or completing class assignments. Then, after a bath and breakfast, I take the 7.30 college special from the corner of our street. We have classes from 8.30 a.m. to 3 p.m. with a short lunch break of forty minutes, when I eat in the college canteen with friends. After classes, it is time for the library where we work until 4 p.m. Later after a wash and a quick snack at home, it is time to go to the music class, which is just ten minutes away. Back home, I study for about two hours, until 9 p.m. Dinner is the nicest part of the day, spent with my parents and sister. Finally, after watching television for about 45 minutes, it is time to go to bed at 10.30.

6. *My idea of a satisfying career*

To begin with, I think it is most important that the work we take up should truly interest us. A satisfying career should offer us enough opportunities for work, that has variety and that is innovative. Personally I would like a career that will allow me to continuously learn and improve my skills. Work that is mechanical, with no scope for any creativity, may soon become boring and monotonous. Further, challenges, and targets and deadlines to be met will spur one on to achieve more. Travelling and meeting people will also add to the joy of an exciting career. Additionally, a career can really be rewarding when there is both acknowledgement and appreciation of the work done as well as a steady rise.

7. *My family*

I am fortunate to be part of a large, noisy, happy family. There is my father, a journalist, and my mother, an engineer with the Kerala State Electricity Board. I am the youngest of three children, and I have an elder brother and sister, both of whom are working. My grandparents live with us, and they enrich our lives with their wisdom, warmth and gentle guidance on all kinds of matters. Although my uncle, aunt and two playful cousins live next door, they are almost always at our house and are very much a part of our family. Together we have a lot of fun, and are there for one another during good as well as bad times.

8. *An experience of performing on stage*

A youth festival is organised by the state government every year, when young people from all parts of the state are selected to take part in a variety of competitions. I was one of the participants in the instrumental music category in the 2006 festival. I was at first very excited, and spent long hours practising on my flute. However, as the date of the competition drew close, I found that I was getting nervous. Of course, my friends and also everyone at home gave me a great deal of support and encouragement. My music teacher in fact proved to be a friend and a critic, and helped me perfect the pieces I was to play. Soon it was the day of the competition, and I found myself seated in an auditorium with other participants and their friends and family. I heard my name being announced as though from a distance, and walked up to the dais on legs that seemed to have turned into jelly. At first I felt a stab of fear when I looked at the audience, but moments after I began playing on the flute, I lost myself completely in its melodious notes. Finally, when the results were announced, I was overjoyed to find that I was placed second in the category.

9. Qualities that draw me to people

All of us find ourselves being attracted to people with qualities we admire. I am especially drawn to persons who are spontaneously warm and concerned about others. It is nice to meet people who are able to respond with affection towards everyone they come in contact with. It is difficult to feel lonely or depressed when such people are by our side. They can be depended on in both good and bad times. Such people make wonderful friends indeed.

10. My goal in life

I am happy that I have a clear goal in life. To me my goal is more than an aim. It is a cherished dream, something that I look forward to achieving every moment of my waking hours. I am going to be a gymnast, and I hope I will do my family and nation proud some day. My parents understand how strong my longing is, and have arranged for me to have professional coaching. I have participated in many district and state level competitions, and won prizes. However, I think my parents are right when they insist that I get an undergraduate degree before I take up gymnastics as a career. I believe in my goal and just know that I will get there.

11. An adventure

Let me tell you about an exciting adventure that I had some days ago. I was on my way back home from college when my motorcycle broke down in the deserted ridge area. Seeing that there was no way to get the vehicle started, I decided to walk through the woods to the main road, from where I could take an autorickshaw or a bus home. I had walked that way many times with friends and did not really feel nervous. Therefore, I was terrified when I found two men appear suddenly from behind a clump of trees, holding thick sticks in their hands. The men asked me to hand over my wallet. But fortunately at that moment, a snake slithered out of a bush near one of the men, and finding that their attention was diverted, I raced through the trees, screaming for help. The thugs came after me and were barely two metres away when I caught sight of the road and some late evening walkers. I quickly scampered up to safety and was dropped home by a cheerful woman and her husband.

12. A memorable day in my life

Something happened when I was eight years old and the memory of it is still clear in my mind. I had been a single child, safe and comfortable in the unconditional love of my parents and all the others in the family. One day, the woman who helped us with the housework died after an illness. She was a widow who lived alone with her baby daughter. My parents thought about the situation and the future of the child, Sushma, and decided to adopt her. They told me about their plan and said that they would bring the two-year-old home only if it was perfectly all right with me. Of course, I thought it would be fun to have a baby at home and hugged my parents in joy. So one day, many months later, I returned from school to find Sushma asleep on my bed. I stood looking down at her until, suddenly, her eyes flew open and she gave me a lop-sided smile. I can never forget the day my little sister was given to me.

13. A person who inspires me

My mathematics teacher is a very special person. I did not really believe that any individual could have a powerful effect on another until I walked into Dr Jaya Sarkar's class. Dr Sarker is a wonderful teacher and mathematician. I have never found a person who can hold a class spellbound with the magic she seemed to create with numbers. In fact, I had never been very enthusiastic about mathematics, but I have become passionate about the subject ever since I started attending Jaya Sarkar's classes. Another reason why I admire her is that she is a woman of remarkable personal qualities, which include compassion and a terrific sense of humour. I am sure Dr Sarkar will remain a constant source of inspiration to me long after she stops being my teacher.

14. My college campus

The Arts College, where I study, has a sprawling campus spread over 6 acres in the middle of the city. The main building is about a hundred years old, and has huge arched corridors and spacious rooms with high ceilings. This has the principal's office, the main administrative office and an auditorium with a wide stage at its far end. The new blocks are modern and airy with large glass windows and light furniture. The classrooms, staff rooms, library, science and computer labs and gymnasium are all in this part of the campus. There is a wide field for football and cricket, and tennis and basketball courts as well. The swimming pool is right next to the tennis court. The most attractive part of the college campus, however, is its beautifully maintained gardens and treelined, shady avenues, where students can relax or take a walk between classes.

15. Something I long to do

I hope to be able to travel round the world some day. Reading about places in India and abroad has filled me with a longing to visit them and to meet the people who live there. I would love to drink in the beauty of the mountains, forests and beaches in the lands I visit, and stroll through their museums and historical monuments. It would be wonderful to be able to see how people live in different places, to enjoy the colours of their dances and costumes, to listen to them speak their languages, and to tap my feet to their music. I would also like to try the local cuisines and, of course, learn to pronounce the names of the dishes I relished most.

Sample paragraphs on general topics

1. The greenhouse effect

The earth is getting warmer. This is because of the greenhouse effect. The sun's rays penetrate the atmosphere, which absorbs some of its heat and reflects the rest back into space. However, now the thick gases produced by human activities trap too much heat and, consequently, the temperature of the earth's atmosphere has been steadily increasing. This increase in temperature will affect all life on the planet. The two main gases responsible for the greenhouse effect are carbon dioxide and methane. Many governments have begun to look at ways of reducing the emissions of greenhouse gases. Some of the steps taken are large scale planting of trees, introducing taxes to be imposed on industries producing the harmful gases, and promoting alternative sources of energy, the generation of which will not produce the harmful gases.

2. Deforestation

Deforestation is the permanent destruction of natural forests and woodlands. The rate at which deforestation is happening is a matter of great concern. The phenomenon is the result of large-scale cutting down of forests in order to make more land available for agriculture, industries and housing. There is also a great demand for wood as both fuel and building material. Widespread deforestation leads to a huge increase in carbon dioxide, which is produced when trees are burnt or allowed to rot. Secondly, with vegetation disappearing from the surface of the earth, there is soil erosion. This is therefore also one of the causes for desertification. Finally, many species are in danger of becoming extinct due to loss of natural habitats. If steps to prevent deforestation are not taken soon, we are likely to lose all our tropical forests in few years from now.

3. The importance of sports

Sports have always had an important place in human society—in prehistoric communities, in ancient civilizations and in the modern world. It is right that this should be so because sports are a healthy means of fulfilling our inherent desire to compete, to establish new records and to be recognised. Sports have come to be especially relevant in present times. First, it is well known that the discipline and physical activity involved keep the people who take up sports strong in mind and body. Our lives today are marked by alarming levels of stress, and participating in and watching sports will help reduce this considerably. Sports also inculcate in people the desirable qualities of team spirit and fair play. Most importantly, however, is the fact that sports bring people together. Thus sports form the single, most effective alternative to war by allowing groups of people to compete for supremacy without violence or bloodshed.

4. Superstitions

Superstitions are 'blind' beliefs that are not based on reason or on the laws of science. They are found in different parts of the world and are handed down from one generation to the next one. For example, it is believed that or the breaking of a mirror or a cat crossing one's path bring bad luck. Similarly, finding a horse shoe is supposed to be a sign of good fortune. Superstitions cannot be proved and we can never be sure if there is any truth in them. However, it is certain that believing fully in them would burden our minds and fill us with either irrational fear or impossible hopes. Both these have a disturbing effect and take away our peace of mind. It is best to treat superstitions simply as interesting beliefs, and carry on with faith in oneself and in life.

5. Euthanasia

Euthanasia is the act of helping a person who is terminally ill to die painlessly. It is considered as an option only when the patient is either in terrible pain and longs for death or is in a prolonged comatose state. Euthanasia may be achieved by administering drugs that would lead to a painless death. It could, on the other hand, simply be the result of taking the patient off all life-support systems, which some doctors may do more readily than killing the patient with the help of a lethal drug. The act is an offence in most countries and has been made legal only in places like Holland and

Belgium. The two sides of the controversy regarding euthanasia involve the conflicting aspects of the right of an individual to die with dignity under a very specific set of circumstances and that of the essential sacredness of life.

6. Education in India

Education in India, at the school and higher levels, is undoubtedly of a high standard. There are many premier institutions in the country offering well-designed courses and having both qualified teaching faculty and excellent infrastructure. However, there are some serious problems in the system, and these need to be resolved. Firstly, the education imparted is most often completely theoretical, with little or no relevance to the demands that would be made on students later, in real working situations. Secondly, although a lot has already been done in the matter, the present examination system in our schools and colleges needs to be replaced by a method of testing students for a fair and accurate assessment of their skills and their understanding of the subjects of study as well as of their ability to apply what they have learnt to real-life situations. Lastly, it is now widely accepted that secondary school education needs to be vocationalised. This will not only help large numbers of students find their true vocations in life but it will also reduce the rush for college education merely for the sake of an academic qualification.

7. Fashion

The term 'fashion' means any trend or style followed by a majority of a community for a given period of time. It applies to not just clothes but also to jewellery, interior design, handicrafts and household goods. Fashion has become a huge, fast-growing industry in the world today. In fact, a fairly large section of consumers now buy clothes and other items created by well-known designers and sold in up-market retail stores. Fashion is often understood to mean what we see models display on the ramp. This, however, is a misconception for that is high fashion, which is not really meant for all sections of the community. Although fashion is most often influenced by trends set by famous personalities, anything that is well-designed, perfectly made, comfortable to use or wear and beautifully displayed will appeal to people with good taste, and soon become 'fashion'.

8. Population control

Over-population is today a very serious problem in many countries of the world, and this includes India. It is closely related to other problems such as food and water shortage, unemployment, overcrowding and lack of basic facilities. Many governments have tried to solve the problem in different ways. Unfortunately, some of the measures adopted are rather extreme, and these have not really been effective in reducing the population in the countries concerned. Thus, it is seen that sterilising by force, having laws restricting the number of children a married couple may have and making larger families a punishable offence are methods that anger people and defeat the purpose altogether. On the contrary, educating people and spreading the message of a small family, improving the conditions of women, especially in rural areas, and making them aware of the advantages of having fewer children, and offering tax rebates and other incentives have proved effective in many parts of the world and in our country as well.

9. Animal rights

Animals have as much a right to live on this planet as we do. It is, therefore, unfortunate that they are treated with shocking cruelty and complete insensitivity by humans. In the course of our exploitation of the earth's land and natural resources, we rob animals of their homes and their means of getting food. Animals are used mercilessly by people for work or for entertainment. They are also killed in large numbers for their meat, skin and fur. These are among the main reasons for the fact that many species of birds and animals have either become extinct or are in danger of being wiped out. It is time we accept that a terrible injustice is being done to animals and stand up to fight for their rights.

10. The issue of reservation

There has been a recent move by the Centre to reserve up to 27 per cent seas in leading educational institutions and government jobs for OBC students. Actually, the issue of reservation is not new or unfamiliar to the people in the country as it has been discussed and debated for over sixty years now. It is true that we need to help the underprivileged by offering them some advantages to make up for all that they have been deprived of until recently. However, what the protesters argue is that having reservation at the school level should be enough to bring the severely disadvantaged sections of our society up to a standard that would allow these people to participate confidently in competitive examinations for entry into premier institutions and government jobs. It is feared that any more reservations would only create a situation where a different group of people would be at a disadvantage, leading again to frustration and anger. What could be an even more serious consequence of introducing reservation at a higher level is that it will divide the youth of the country and create in them extreme tension and a feeling of being wronged.

11. Environmental pollution

There are different forms of environmental pollution. Air pollution is caused by the burning of coal and oil. It can damage the earth's vegetation and cause respiratory problems in humans. A second type of pollution is noise pollution. It is the result of the noise of aeroplanes and heavy traffic. Further, loud music is also a cause of noise pollution, which has been seen to affect people's hearing and give them severe headaches and high blood pressure. Another source of pollution is radioactivity, which occurs when there is a leak from a nuclear power station. Radioactivity is a deadly pollutant that has been known to kill and cause irreparable harm to those exposed to it. Land and water pollution are caused by huge quantities of rubbish, sewage and chemical wastes that are disposed thoughtlessly. Lastly, pollution of rivers and seas kills fishes and other marine life and also becomes the cause for water-borne diseases.

12. The place of English in today's world

English is spoken by people in almost all parts of the world today. While the language is their mother tongue for people in the UK, the USA, Australia and Canada, English is taught as a second language in India and many African countries. In the latter situation, English happens to be the most common medium of higher education and official work. Further, in many multilingual countries where it is used as a second language, English is the most widely used language of communication among the speakers of different languages. It is also the major language of mass communication, of business and commerce, and of computers and the World Wide Web. Thus, English has come to occupy an important place in the present world.

13. Fusion dance

Fusion dance is becoming an art form in its own right. More and more classical dancers all over the world are adapting the classical dances in their countries to incorporate the themes and styles of dance forms of other cultures. Many young dancers today are no longer satisfied with themes traditionally dealt with and look at ways of expressing contemporary themes through their art. Dancers experimenting with fusion dance forms do not disown the traditions of their own dance forms, but work in features of other dance forms and include costumes that are contemporary. Senior dancers such as Ananda Shankar and younger artistes like Yamini Reddy have presented fusion dance items that cross all barriers of race, culture, religion and nationality.

14. Cloning

Cloning is one of the major breakthroughs of the late twentieth century in the field of genetic engineering. The first cloned animal, Dolly, was created in 1997 in Scotland. The method used is nuclear transfer, where the nucleus of a cell is isolated and implanted into an 'empty' egg. The egg is made to start growing with the help of an electric spark. It is then transferred to another animal, which in due course gives birth to a cloned young one. Although the technique is being used by scientists to clone plants and animals, cloning is a fiercely debated issue when it concerns human beings. In spite of its apparent benefits to humanity, such as for example, removing chances of genetically inherited diseases, there are many people who believe that cloning human beings would be unethical and would lead to horrifying consequences. The debate continues with some countries asking that the practice be banned while others argue that cloning could simply be regulated. This led to the UN General Assembly's decision in November 2003 to delay a ban on cloning by two years.

15. Child labour

The practice of employing young children, a shameful blot on civilised human society, is still being followed in many parts of the world. In our country, for example, in spite of the framing of laws meant to protect the rights of children, it is sad to find thousands of children working for long hours under the blazing sun in agricultural fields, in dark and airless mines and in the midst of explosive fireworks. The government has indeed tried hard to prevent the exploitation of children by making education free and compulsory up to the age of fourteen and by introducing the mid-day meal programme in schools all over the country. In spite of this, children continue to be made to work mainly because of the poverty and illiteracy of their parents and the low wages that they need to be paid. A permanent solution to the problem can be found only by getting more people involved in the fight against child labour, by making the laws more effective and by educating parents about the rights of their children.

Exercise

Write paragraphs of five or six sentences on each of the following topics. Remember to follow the steps suggested above for writing coherent paragraphs.

1. Solar energy
2. The importance of celebrations in our lives
3. Wildlife conservation
4. A decision that changed my life
5. Human values are timeless and eternal
6. A meaningful education

7. On being a member of a global community
8. Advantages of vegetarianism
9. An exciting holiday
10. Cherishing old people
11. My favourite cuisine
12. Terrorism: irrational and inhumane

Report Writing

A report is a piece of writing that, as the name suggests, presents a 'report', or information on an event, situation or process. A report must, on account of its primary purpose, be written in clear, simple language and in a direct style that would help the person for whom it is meant find the required information quickly and easily. It is necessary to be clear about three things when writing a report—what the report is about, who it is meant for and what it will be used for.

Reports are of three kinds. These are newspaper reports, reports of scientific experiments and processes that were carried out, and official reports that are prepared on the instructions of someone in authority. Let us first look at some features and samples of newspaper reports.

Newspaper Reports and General Reports

Newspaper reports cover current events and everyday incidents in the country and abroad that would be of interest to its readers. They deal with a variety of subjects such as education, entertainment, commerce and industry, politics, sports, science and stories of human interest. Reports for newspapers consist of a direct presentation of facts relating to some situation or event. They are generally impersonal and objective in style. What this means is that the writer of such a report or the editor simply presents facts as objectively as possible, without expressing their own reactions to the incidents. Some characteristic features of newspaper reports are listed below. You would find it useful to refer to these when writing a newspaper report either as an examination task or for publication in a newspaper.

- The verb in the headings of newspaper reports is either in simple present tense or in past participle form. Sometimes the verb appears in the 'to + verb stem' form, which is referred to as the infinitive.

  Karnataka *agrees* to share river water
  England *beats* Denmark
  Three teachers *awarded* Bharat Ratna
  Kendriya Vidyalaya *to play* in football final tournament

- Factual descriptions and narrations in newspaper reports use a mixture of active and passive voice. This choice is made on the basis of whether the performer of the action is important and needs to be focused on, whether the performer of the action is understood, is not really relevant, is not known or whose identity needs to be kept a secret.

  The prime minister met the members of the visiting UN committee last evening. The meeting was arranged in the Parliament House Annexe. It is believed that immediate plans to fight terrorism were discussed at the meeting.

  The first sentence in the report is in active voice with the doer of the act of 'meeting' in subject position. This is because it is important for the reader to know who met the members of the committee. The second sentence is in passive voice because it is not important to identify the person(s) who oversaw the arrangements of the meeting. The third sentence is again in passive voice because it may cause trouble to reveal the source of the information regarding the subject of the meeting.

- Newspaper reports also often include the opinions and statements by important persons, experts or those in authority. These may be either in reported speech or in the exact words of the speaker, in direct speech enclosed in inverted commas. Some newspaper reports are seen to use both direct and indirect speech to express the comments and views of others.

> The head of the cardiology unit at M. R. L. Hospital confirmed reports that the patient is in a critical condition. Dr Prabhat Kumar said, 'The patient has been put on a ventilator following a massive cardiac arrest. His kidneys, liver and lungs too are not functioning satisfactorily.'

The first sentence in the report above is in indirect speech while the second is in direct speech. There are some specific reporting verbs that are commonly found in newspaper reports. Some of these are: 'called upon', 'deplored', 'praised', 'declined', 'condemned', 'urged', 'exhorted', 'foresaw' and 'denied'.

- A fourth feature of newspaper reports is the use of the expressions 'unconfirmed/confirmed reports' and 'reliable sources' as in the following extracts from newspaper reports.

> There have been *confirmed reports* of heavy shelling in several areas of the city. According to *reliable sources,* the woman writer has been nominated for the Sahitya Kala Parishad award for the year 2006.

Such expressions are used either in the absence of an authentic source of information or when there is a need to keep the identity of the official or source confidential.

Sometimes you are asked to write a factual report (not necessarily meant to be published in a newspaper) describing an event or situation. Your report, in which you will describe an event, such as a cultural programme or trip, is meant to capture in words the most important details of the event. Although these reports are written with the same purpose as newspaper reports—to convey information on a happening—general reports are not as formal in style as those written for the newspaper.

Note that reports, meant for the newspaper or those written for the college magazine or as a class assignment, usually consist of more than one paragraph. The report in such cases begins with an introductory paragraph where basic information regarding the venue, date and time of the event reported is given. The next two or three paragraphs are used to describe the event in more detail.

The final paragraph sums up or concludes the report. Look at the following samples of both newspaper and general reports. The lengths of four of the samples below have deliberately been limited to a single paragraph for reasons of space.

Sample reports

1. Landslide in Uttaranchal claims fifty-six lives

Following heavy rains for the last one week, an entire hillside in Chopta collapsed and came rolling down in the early hours of Monday morning. There were about twenty stone and mud houses on the hill, which had plantations of fruit trees and vegetables and small dairy farms as well. The heavy loss to life and property occurred mainly because people were asleep when the disaster struck. 'We are completely shattered,' sobbed an old farmer who was among the many people in the village to have lost their homes, loved ones, crops and property. Within minutes of the landslide, the district administration swung into action and steps were taken to provide medical care, food and shelter to those affected. The chief minister discussed the situation with the district collector and announced the payment of a sum of Rs. 100 000 to each of the families affected.

2. Communal riot in Vilaspuram

The small sleepy town of Vilaspuram was the scene of a serious communal riot on Tuesday, 22 May 2006. The incident that sparked off the violent clash between two communities was the local municipal authority's refusal to permit a religious procession to pass through the Vasant Bagh locality. Members of the two dominant communities in the town hurled stones at each other and burnt down cars and buses. Manoj, a youth leader, accused the government of trying to provoke a clash between the two communities that had lived together peacefully for very long. Police, however, were able to bring the situation under control within a short time after the clash began. About twenty persons were arrested and the injured were rushed to hospital. No deaths have been reported.

3. KSP's political rally a success

The KSP party's rally held in the East Fort grounds in Thiruvananthapuram on Friday proved to be a huge success. Hundreds of party workers and supporters from outside the city gathered at the venue of the event to demonstrate their support to the party. Party president, P. Rajan, party general secretary, Lailamma Jacob, and leader of the KSP's youth wing, Mukundan Nair, all addressed the rally and spoke of the present political situation in the state as well as in the country. The leaders also expressed their opinions on current concerns and issues affecting the lives of people. The rally was conducted in a peaceful manner and discipline was maintained all through the event. At the end of the rally, the crowds dispersed quietly while the hundred policemen and women on duty stood by in silence.

4. Earthquake in Bilaspur

The small sleepy town of Bilaspur was destroyed completely when an earthquake struck without warning at 2.15 a. m. on 2 June 2006. The damage caused by the earthquake was immense. Two hundred people were killed and more than twice the number were reported to have been badly injured. Most of the buildings in the town collapsed and the railway lines connecting Bilaspur to the outside world were wrecked. There was total power breakdown with the transmission lines being snapped. The earthquake, measuring 5 on the Richter scale, was more powerful than any experienced in the area. It uprooted trees and left huge crevices in the streets of the town. Even hours after the earthquake, slight tremors were felt in some parts of the town.

The army was called out to assist the local administration in its relief operations. Furthermore, several NGOs and other voluntary organisations came forward to pull out the dead and injured from under the debris of buildings, provide medical assistance, food, water and shelter. The chief minister accompanied by the police commissioner and other senior officials in the state visited Bilaspur to assess the situation. An amount of Rs 4 crore is being released from the chief ministers fund, and this would be used to pay a compensation of 1 lakh to each of the affected families and also to take care of at least a part of the expenses incurred in providing relief to the victims.

5. A trip to Pondicherry

During the summer vacation this year, we went in a large group consisting of four families to Pondicherry. We travelled from Chennai by bus along the scenic East Coast Road. The drive, which took us three hours, was just wonderful and all along we could smell the tang of the sea and see the waves come racing to the shore.

Pondicherry is a charming town that was once a French colony. We booked into a quiet, old-fashioned hotel very close to the Beach Road facing the Bay of Bengal. The road is also part of the city's French Quarter and is a good place to stroll leisurely and enjoy a scenic view of the sea. Our first impression of Pondicherry was that of a clean, well-planned town with imposing French-style buildings. The local people prefer to cycle or walk about the town and so there is very little traffic and noise on the roads. On the other side of the town is the traditional Tamil quarter with its narrow streets and traditional houses with elaborately carved doorways. The shops were filled with the usual artefacts and souvenirs, but I was especially delighted by the stalls selling brilliantly coloured flowers.

We visited the Pondicherry Museum, filled with interesting Chola, Roman and French exhibits. Two other attractions for tourists are the 19th century Church of Our Lady of the Angels and Raj Nivas, which used to be the official residence of an the French governor of Pondicherry, Joseph Dupleix. On the last day of our stay in the city we visited the Aurobindo Ashram with its memorials to the great spiritual leader Sri Aurobindo Ghose and his disciple, better known as the Mother. We spent every moment we could on the warm, golden beaches or shopping in the quaint, tiny stores or enjoying French food in the little cafes that can be found everywhere. Finally, it was time to return home, and we left Pondicherry with happy memories of its friendly people, the warm sand and water, the delicately flavoured cuisine and the sweet smells and sounds of an enchanting place.

6. Activities of the Arts College debating club

The Arts College has a very active debating club. The club is as old as the college itself and follows the tradition of having the Head of the English Department as its president. A student from the final year is chosen every year to be the secretary of the club.

The debating club organises many debating events. First, there are the inter-class debates held once a month where students are allowed to suggest topics for the debate and the final topic is selected by a draw of lots. The winners of the inter-class debates are given training to improve their debating skills and sent out to other colleges for competitions. The debating club also holds an annual debating event in which other educational institutions are invited to participate. The event is considered to be prestigious and so attracts a large number of participants, making it necessary to spread the competitions over three days. Finally, the college is a member of the All India Debating Society and sends its debaters to represent the college in the major competitions organised by the society.

The annual debate for this year is being held next month at the Gandhi Memorial Hall. The topic for the debate will be announced two days before the competition. Student members and teachers associated with the club are busy finalising arrangements for the big event in which over sixty debaters from different colleges in the state are expected to take part.

7. Inter-college dance competition

The inter-college dance competition, *Nrityanjali*, was held in the university convocation hall at 6 p.m. on 18 April 2006. The competition, in which twenty colleges participated, was judged by a panel comprising noted dancers Bharati Shivaji, Sonal Mansingh and Raja Reddy. The chief guest for the evening was Prabhakar Rao, Minister of State for Education, who spoke briefly on keeping alive the cultural traditions of the nation.

The items presented in the solo section included bharatanatyam, odissi, mohini attam and kuchipudi styles. Among the group dances presented by students of six colleges were bhangra, kaikottikali and bamboo dance. The variety and colours of the costumes, the graceful movements of the dancers, the sparkle of jewelry and the tinkling of anklets had a mesmerising effect on the audience. The music, vocal and instrumental, accompanying the dances was of a high standard and added to the beauty of the performances.

The first prize in the solo section was awarded to Hemalata of the Kottayam Government Science College for her odissi performance. The second and third prizes went to Akshay and Shubha of the College of Architecture and Women's College, Cheruthuruthi for their bharatanatyam and mohini attam performances respectively. The bhangra group dance presented by students of the Kozhikode Medical College was judged the best in its category because of the vigour, fluid grace and rhythm with which it was performed.

The function concluded with a short ceremony in which the chief guest gave away the prizes. The secretary of the organising committee presented bouquets and mementos to the chief guest and to the members of the committee. Finally, a vote of thanks was proposed by the president of the Kerala University Students' Union, Joe Abraham.

8. *Encouraging employment trends in the IT sector in India*

According to Nasscom, the premier trade body and voice of the IT software and service industry in India, job opportunities in the sector will touch an all-time high in the months ahead. The total IT software and services employment is estimated to reach 1,287,000 by the end of 2006. It is reported that the industry has already initiated several measures to find suitable talent for the industry in the country. One of these is the development of comprehensive skill assessment and certification programmes for entry-level professionals and for middle-level executives. Also being planned is an image enhancement programme that would help create greater awareness about career opportunities in the field. Finally, it is understood that Nasscom is working with academics all over the country in order to encourage and facilitate greater interaction with the industry. All this, it is hoped, will lead to a great increase in opportunities for employment for fresh IT graduates.

Reports of experiments and processes

Writing reports of experiments and processes involves a different style from that used in newspaper reports and general, descriptive reports. Since reports of scientific experiments need to focus on the procedure rather than the performer of the experiment, the verb appears in passive voice all through the report. This is also true of reports of cooking processes written, for example, in a hotel management class. Thus, in the following pairs of sentences, the second sentence would be more appropriate than the first one for recording the steps of an experiment conducted in the laboratory or for reporting how a dish was made in a cookery class.

The student *took* 5 ml of hydrochloric acid in a glass tube.
5 ml of hydrochloric acid *was taken* in a glass tube.

The chef *marinated* the fish slices in a paste of onions, ginger and garlic.
The fish slices *were marinated* in a paste of onions, ginger and garlic.

Reports of scientific experiments usually arrange their information under the following headings.

Aim
Apparatus
Principle
Procedure
Observations
Conclusions

Here, however, we will be learning to report mainly the procedures followed and the observations made in scientific reporting, and just the procedures followed in reporting cooking and other kinds of processes. Look at the samples below. The first two are reports of completed scientific experiments while the third sample is a report of the steps followed in making a dish.

Sample reports

1. A saucepan of water *was kept* on a tripod stand. A spirit lamp *was placed* under it and *lighted*. When the water began to boil, a metal spoon and a wooden spoon *were placed* in the water with their handles projecting outside the water. The spoons *were left* in the boiling water for two minutes. The handle of the metal spoon *was felt* with the left hand and the handle of the wooden spoon with the right hand. It *was found* that the handle of the metal spoon felt hotter to the touch than that of the wooden spoon. It was *proved* that metal conducts heat better than wood.

2. A can with a duct for excess liquid to overflow *was taken*. The can *was filled* with water to the level of the duct. An irregular object *was put* in the can and the displaced water *collected* in a collecting can. The volume of the water that overflowed *was measured*. This *was found* to be equal to the volume of the irregular object that was put into the water.

3. A tablespoon of cooking oil *was heated* in a pressure cooker. Cardamoms, cloves and finely sliced onions, and a teaspoonful of ginger-garlic paste *were added* to the hot oil and *sautéed* until golden brown. A cup of washed and drained rice together with chopped carrots, beans and capsicums *was put* into the pressure cooker and *stirred* for a few minutes. Two cups of water *were poured* into the mixture of rice and vegetables and half a teaspoon of salt *was added*. The lid of the pressure cooker *was closed* tight, and when steam began to escape, a weight *was placed* on the vent. The gas stove *was turned off* after one whistle, and the pressure cooker *was allowed* to cool before being opened.

Official reports

Official reports are formal reports written in response to instructions received from persons in authority. They are also referred to as 'survey reports' because the writer of such a report often has to study a situation or conduct an investigation on the matter concerned before submitting the report. It is essential for these reports to present facts clearly and concisely because they will be used to take decisions. A formal report usually has the following format.

1. From: (name and designation of the person writing the report)
2. Date
3. To: (name and designation of the person to whom the report is sent)
4. Title of the report
5. Terms of reference (who authorised the report/why it is being made, what the reporter has been asked to survey, etc.)
6. Abstract or summary (included when the report is very long, so that busy senior colleagues may get the essence of the report quickly, without having to go through the main body of the report)
7. Body of the report (containing the findings of the investigation)
8. Conclusion (containing the reporter's interpretation of the facts, and his/her comments and recommendations)
9. Signature of the person writing the report

Look at the sample given below for an illustration of the format that has been suggested for official reports.

From:
Dr S. P. Unni
Assistant Medical Officer
District Health Centre
Thrissur

Date: 14 June 2006

To:
Dr Mehtab Akhtar
Chief Medical Officer
District Health Centre
Thrissur

Title: Deaths due to dengue fever

Terms of reference: As instructed by the Minister of State for Health, a survey was conducted to investigate the reports received of over thirty people dying of dengue fever in four villages in the district.

Findings: The writer visited the four villages of Attoor, Plakode, Killimangalam and Panjal to confirm the above reports and study the situation. The findings of the study are as follows.

a. According to records maintained in the local government hospitals as well as in private nursing homes, the number of patients diagnosed with dengue fever was 23 in Attoor, 14 in Plakode, 22 in Killimangalam and 30 in Panjal.
b. While 19 patients suffered from mild forms of the fever, 70 patients presented acute symptoms and needed hospitalisation.
c. The line of treatment followed was in accordance with that recommended for the management of dengue fever.
d. 40 deaths were confirmed by the hospital and local panchayats.
e. For more than two weeks now, no fresh cases of dengue have been reported.

Conclusion and recommendations: The outbreak of dengue fever appears to have been brought under control before it became an epidemic. It is recommended that the primary health care centres in the district keep a close watch on the condition of the other patients suffering from the fever and report other deaths if any. Further, the centres should be instructed to immediately alert the District Health Centre if new cases of dengue fever were reported in the area.

S. P. Unni
(Dr S. P. Unni)

Exercise 1

Write brief newspaper reports of two paragraphs each on the following topics.

a. A railway accident
b. Traffic congestion
c. An international football/cricket match
d. A major archaeological discovery
e. New shopping mall
f. Inauguration of theme park
g. New superfast bus from Bangalore to Pune
h. Flash floods in Orissa
i. Amjad Ali Khan honoured
j. Student politics

Exercise 2

Write reports of three short paragraphs each on the following topics for your college magazine.

a. Annual drama festival
b. College union elections
c. English literary club
d. A bus ride to Ooty
e. Temple festival
f. Visit to a historical monument
g. Id-ul-fitr celebrations
h. Tree plantation week
i. Sports day
j. Student exchange programmes

Exercise 3

Imagine that you have completed doing the following experiments/processes. Report, in a paragraph each, the steps followed in doing them.

a. A report on a science experiment of your choice
b. A report on making chapatis/an omlette/vegetable soup

c. A report on dressing a bleeding wound on the foot
d. A report on planting a tulsi sapling in your garden
e. A report on writing a paragraph

Exercise 4

Imagine that you are an education officer with the Kerala Board of Secondary Education. You have been asked by the secretary of the board to investigate rumours of cheating in three examination centres during the 2006 board examinations. Write an official report, presenting facts and making recommendations.

Letter Writing

Letters are an important means of communication. Even though in the present times, electronic mails are more common than letters sent by post, the different types of letters that we write as well as their basic formats and styles remain much the same, except of course on minor points characteristic of the email mode.

Letters, as you would know, can be classified into two major types—personal letters and official letters, which are also referred to as business letters. The formats and a few samples of the two types of letters are given below. We will also look at the structure as well as a sample of an email letter.

Personal letters

Personal letters, as the name suggests, are written to friends and relatives. Their tone is therefore personal and the style used informal or, sometimes, even conversational. Personal letters could be about your home, family, work or something interesting that happened to you. Thus, a letter written to a classmate describing the farewell party that she could not attend and a letter written to your uncle enquiring about his health are examples of personal letters. Look at the letter below.

No. 12 Staff Quarters
CCMB Campus
Habsiguda
Hyderabad 500 075

15 July 2006

Dear Shoma,

Thank you for the lovely greeting card. It was nice of you to remember my birthday and find time to buy a card too.

How are things at your end? You must be very busy with classes at college. It is wonderful that you are happy doing architecture. I am so glad you opted for the course in spite of all the doubts you had before enrolling in it. You will design a house for me free some day, won't you?

How are your parents and grandfather? They must be missing your brother terribly. By the way, Vilas called me last month when he was passing through Hyderabad—he has threatened to visit us next time he is here!

We are all well. Ma is a little busy with her PhD students. Baba has been travelling more than he usually has to do and just refuses to stir out on days when he is in town. Prema has realised (about time she did!) that she will have to work very hard over the next few months if she is to achieve her dream of becoming an IPS officer. Everybody here sends you their love.

I must stop now. Please convey my affectionate regards to your parents and grandfather. I shall ask my parents if I can make a short trip to Kolkata during the winter break.

Yours affectionately,

Jyoti

A personal letter has six parts. These are marked for you in the figure on the next page. Let us look at the parts one by one.

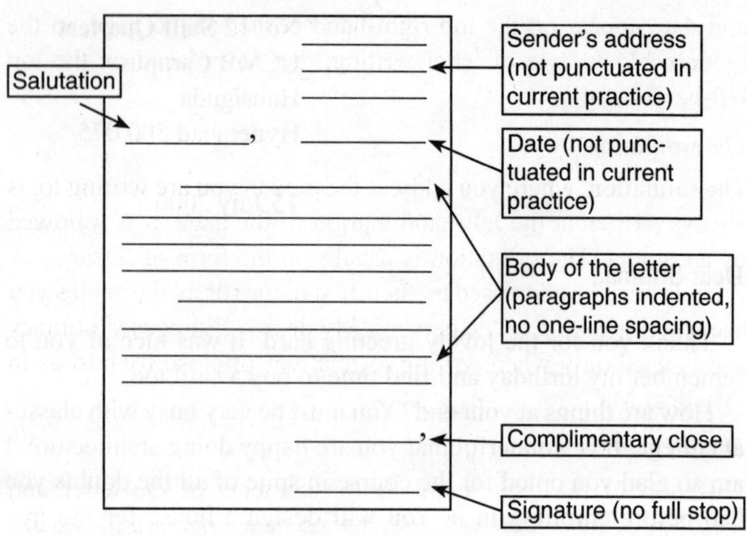

The sender's address

If there has been a recent change in your address or if you are writing to a person for the first time, your complete address must be given. If you do not live in the same country as the person you are writing to, it is suggested that you write the name of the country you are writing from. The address of the person you are writing to (the 'inside address') need not be given in a personal letter.

The date

The date on which the letter is written comes below the sender's address, with a blank line separating the two. There are many ways of writing the date, though according to current practice, there is no comma between the year and the rest of the date, as in '6 March 2006'. (In countries like the USA, which follow the month-date-year system, a comma is used between the date and the year, as in, 'March 6, 2006'.) Note that the use of suffixes *–th, -nd* and *–st* with dates is no longer favoured, while forms like, '6/3/'06' or '6.3.2006' are not used because they lead to ambiguity in some countries, where it would be understood as 3 June instead of 6 March. Although in the traditional format, the sender's address and date appear on the top right-hand corner of the page, in the modern block style of letter writing, they are placed on the top left-hand margin.

The salutation

The salutation, where you address the person you are writing to, is always written at the left-hand margin of the page. It is followed by a comma. The salutation is usually in the form of 'Dear . . .'. Friends must be addressed by their first names or by the names you use when speaking to the person. 'My dear . . .' suggests intimacy and is used only when writing to relatives or close friends, as in 'My dear Ma'.

The body of the letter

This part of the letter contains the contents of the letter and it follows the rules of punctuation and paragraph breaks recommended for general writing. In the traditional format, paragraphs are indented and begin five spaces from the left-hand margin. However, paragraphs are not indented in the block style and in this case, they are separated by a one-line space. The best personal letters are those written in the sender's own words, in an easy, spontaneous style.

The complimentary close

In letters using the traditional format, the complimentary close is written on the right-hand side, below the body of the letter, and it is followed by a comma. (In the block style, the complimentary close as well as all the other parts appear at the left-hand margin.) The most commonly used closing phrases in letters to very close friends and relatives are 'Yours affectionately' (but 'Your loving') or just 'Affectionately' or 'Love'. (Note that there is no apostrophe in 'Yours'.) When writing personal letters to people whom you do not know very well, the closing expressions 'Yours sincerely' and 'Sincerely' are preferred.

The signature

The signature of the person writing the letter comes below the complimentary close. You need write only your first name or

Senders add.

Date

Inside add.

Salutation

.

?

Compli. close

Name & Sign.

Block format

Senders add.

Date

Inside add.

Salutation ,

.

?

Compli. close ,

Name & Sign.

Modified block format

Senders add.

Date

Inside add.

Salutation ,

.

?

Compli. close ,

Name & Sign.

Modified semi-block format

the name by which you are known to the person addressed. For example, a signature in a personal letter can be 'Prabhakar' or 'Prabha', and not 'Prabhakar Kumar Sinha'.

Three different formats are currently used in writing letters. These are the block style, the modified block style and the modified semi-block style that are illustrated for you in the figures on the facing page. Personal letters are written in all three formats, depending on individual choice.

Samples of personal letters

1. A letter written to your mother from hostel

My dear Amma,

Surprised to get a letter from me? I know I did speak to you just two days ago, but I felt a sudden urge to write to you. Telephone conversations are never completely satisfying because I usually forget most of what I want to say.

How are you? I hope the backache is not bad any longer with the yoga exercises. Does Kamala come in everyday to help you with the chores at home? She is such a dear, isn't she? Achan spoke to me from Nagpur yesterday. He sounded thrilled about the new engineering project and said that he hoped to be back home on Saturday night. Ravi must be busy preparing for his final examination. Do ask him to send me the CDs he was telling me about.

I am perfectly happy here. As I told you when we spoke on the telephone, I am studying hard. I also spend an hour on the basketball court everyday. Two of my poems have been accepted for the college magazine. In spite of all that, I can't wait to come home for Onam. Take good care of yourself.

Love to all of you,

Kartika

2. A letter to a friend giving her some information she had asked you for

Dear Alice,

I am sorry about not writing to you earlier. Actually, father's doctor friend was not in town and so I could get the information you wanted only last night. Dr Valsan looked at the CT scan reports as well as the results of the other tests. He also discussed your aunt's case with his colleagues in the hospital. They all think that the tumour is benign, but that it would be best to have it removed without any delay. Dr Valsan suggests that your aunt get the surgery done at the KMC Cancer research Centre in Pune. One of his friends, Dr Vinita Pai, is a senior surgeon there, and he offered to speak to her about your aunt. In fact, you could speak to Dr Valsan yourself, if you want to. His landline number is 24107971, and his mobile number is 09869460131.

We are all fine. It's getting very hot here. My parents are going to Patna to attend a relative's wedding. Madhu and I are very excited about staying alone at home for a week.

Hope you are not letting your aunt's illness depress you. Don't worry, she's going to be fine. I shall try to speak to you sometime next week. Please convey my regards to everyone at home.

Affectionately,

Salil

3. A letter written to your uncle congratulating him on his promotion

My dear Mama,

We were delighted to hear that you have been promoted and have now become the principal of your school. Congratulations! You really deserve the position for your selfless efforts all these years. I am sure your students are very happy.

How is Mami's health? When is she getting transferred back to Lucknow? Nalini has not written to me for very long. I guess she must be busy with work as well as with the little ones. Please convey my regards to her and to Mami.
With love and best wishes,

Anju

4. An informal invitation

Dear Sarita,

I am having a small party at home at 5 o'clock tomorrow evening. It is Appu's birthday, and I would like you to come with Nitin and Anu. I really hope you will be able to make it.

Affectionately,

Shreya

5. A letter of condolence

Dear Mr Pillai,

I was shocked and grieved to hear that your sister, Ms Shyamala Chandran, passed away two days ago, and wish to offer my condolences. Your sister was loved by everybody who knew her for her warmth, kindness and wonderful sense of humour. I pray for Ms Chandran's soul and also that you be given the strength to bear this terrible loss.

Yours sincerely,

Shanta D'Souza

6. Letter written to accept an invitation

Dear Amir,

Thank you for inviting me to join you and your cousin on your trip to Kodaikanal. I would love to go with you. You know how I have always wanted to visit a hill station, and besides, being between projects at work, it is really the right time to take a break. I will call you on Friday evening and we'll then talk about the details.

Hope all is well at home. Do convey my regards to Chachaji, Chachiji and Sameena.

Love,

Harpreet

7. Letter written to decline an invitation

Dear Roja,

Thank you for the invitation to Aman's wedding reception on 25 August. I am so happy for all of you, and especially so for Aman. I remember meeting Nandita at my sister's place two years ago. She is a lovely person and I am sure she and Aman will be very happy together.

Roja, I wouldn't have missed the reception if I could have helped it, but Venkat is still in hospital after the heart surgery. He is improving, but doctors want him to be in hospital for another week. I am sorry, but I won't be able to attend the reception. I know you will be terribly disappointed and hope that you understand the situation I am in. Please convey our very best wishes (and apologies!) to Aman and Nandita.

Sincerely,

Lalita

8. A letter written to ask a favour of somebody

My dear Alex,

How are you? I tried to call you a few minutes ago, but couldn't get you at home or on your mobile.

I have a problem and would be grateful if you could do me a favour. All my original certificates and testimonials are with the company I used to work for in Ghaziabad, Punjab Agro Industries. Now my new office here has asked me to submit the certificates in a week's time. Could you go across to the PAI office, collect the certificates and send them by speed post, please. I spoke to the manager in the Personnel Department there, and she says she will hand over the certificates to you. I know this is going to be a bother, but I can't think of any other way of getting the certificates by the end of the week. Thank you, in advance.

Affectionately,

Varun

9. A letter of apology

My dear Hussain,

I am writing to tell you how sorry I am about losing my temper when you came home to see me yesterday. I have been feeling miserable since then. I realise that I behaved very badly, and want to explain that I was very upset on that day because everything had gone wrong for me since morning. It seemed to me that there was nobody who understood my problems or was willing to help me. So when you dropped in to suggest that I go with you to Rahul's party, I simply lost control for a few minutes. I apologise for my rude behaviour and hope you will forgive me. We have been friends for so very long, and I cannot imagine losing you.

Yours affectionately,

Soman

10. A letter written to thank a friend

Dear Gurveen,

Priya and I reached Ottapalam safe this morning. Both father and mother were relieved to hear that Priya's counselling went well and that she has been admitted to the electrical and communication engineering stream in the JNTU there.

Gurveen, I would like you to know that I am grateful for all the help and support we got from you while we were in Hyderabad. As I told you, father was very worried about sending Priya and me alone, but had to do so because neither he nor mother could leave home with the construction work going on. It was really very nice of you to take the trouble to receive and see us off at the railway station, take us home and also accompany us to the counselling centre. Priya and I enjoyed the two days we stayed with your family–all of you did everything you could to make us feel at home. Again, thank you very much!

Hope everybody at home is well. Have the dates of the campus placement programme in your college been confirmed? Best wishes from all of us here. We are sure you will get selected by one of the good software companies. Please convey our regards to your parents.

Affectionately,

Nirmala

Exercise

1. Imagine that you are Nafisa Banu. Write a letter to your aunt telling her about a study tour you went on with teachers and classmates.
2. As Bhushan Bose, write a letter to your friend inviting him/her to your brother's wedding.
3. Imagine that you are Ratna Shetty. Write to your sister Neeru, who is away in hostel, asking her to help you with a presentation when she is home on vacation.
4. You are Ms Vandana John and you have recently moved to Coimbatore. Write to Mr Mukundan Poduval, your neighbour in Rourkela, enquiring after his health. Also, ask about his family and your common friends there.

5. Write a letter to a friend apologising for losing her book. You are S. D. Jebah of Nagercoil.
6. You are Sunny. Write a letter to your cousin congratulating her on getting selected as a copy-editor with the Indian Express.
7. As Fatima Begum, write a letter to your grandfather, telling him of your plan to visit him and your grandmother on Id-ul-fitr.
8. Imagine that you are Navjot Desai and that you are travelling from your home in Chandigarh to Bangalore to attend an interview. Write to your friend Maria's mother requesting her to have you received at the railway station.
9. You are Shyam Sunder. Write a condolence letter to your classmate whose brother died in a road accident.
10. Write a letter to your father, who has been transferred to another city, giving him news about everybody at home and urging him to stay cheerful and take care of his health. You are Benny Matthew of Palakkad.

Official letters

An official letter, as the name suggests, is written to a person in a company or an organisation for some work-related or business purpose. Examples of official letters are those written as part of business transactions, application letters, letters of enquiry, letters to the editor and letters written to one's colleagues on matters concerning work. Look at the official letter below.

B 3/21, Green Park Extn
New Delhi 100 016
Tel. No. 26485332

30 July 2006

The Sales Manager
Pee Kay Pvt Ltd
5 Kanchan Towers

Barakhamba Road
New Delhi 100 001
Dear Sir/Madam,

Subject: Appointment for consultation

I am planning to invest in the stock market and am looking for some professional advice. The name of your company was recommended to me by a friend who is also one of your regular clients.

I would be grateful if you could let me know when it would be convenient for me to meet someone in this connection in your office. Any day of the week, Monday through Friday, would suit me. As for the time, I would prefer that you fix the meeting after 3 p.m.

I look forward to hearing from you soon.

Yours faithfully,

George Fernandes
(Colonel George Fernandes)

You can see from the sample given above that official letters are different from personal letters in the style in which they are written and in their form as well. Official letters have more parts than personal letters. The figure on the next page will give you a fairly good idea of their structure. Note that not all the parts that you see in the figure appear always in official letters. The ones that are not a feature of all official letters have been placed in parentheses.

The figure on the next page shows a traditional format. Official letters today are written in the block or modified block formats presented earlier on in the section. However, unlike personal letters, which are written in all three formats, according to the choice of the person writing the letter, the block format is usually preferred in writing official letters. The seven parts found in every official letter are as follows.

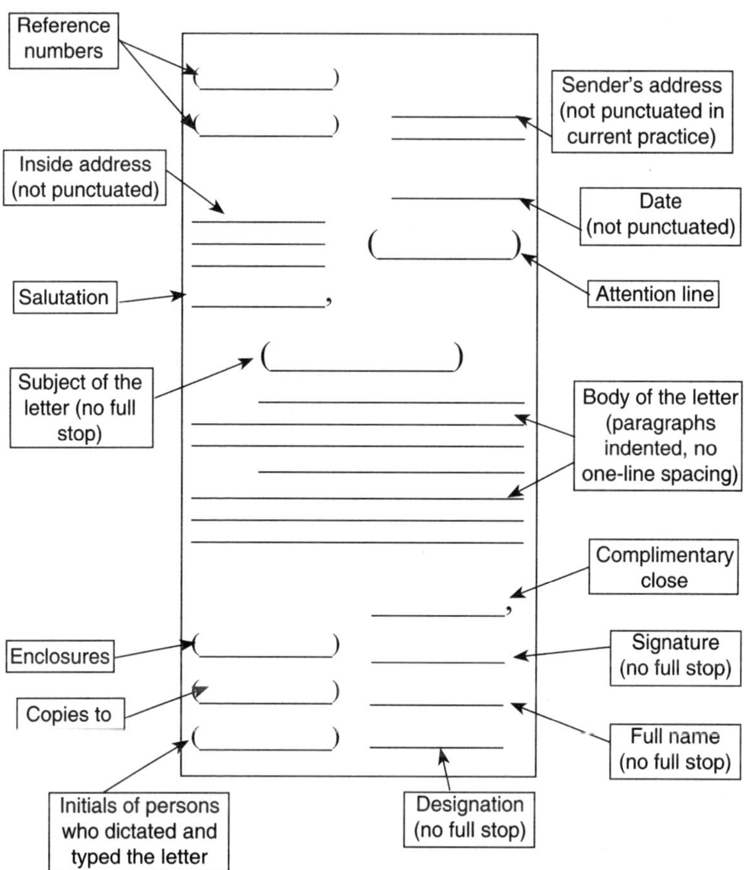

The sender's address

The address of the sender is placed on the right- or left-hand corner of the page depending on the format used. As in the case of personal letters, the address is not punctuated in current practice. It is omitted when official letters are written on company letterheads.

The date

The date, again, is placed below the sender's address as in personal letters.

The inside address

This is the address of the receiver and it is placed on the left, below the line of the date. The inside address is not punctuated, and each line of the address begins on the left margin.

The salutation

The most common forms of salutation in an official letter are 'Dear Sir' (or 'Dear Sirs' if the organisation and not a specific individual is being addressed) and 'Dear Madam'. In case you do not know whether the person to whom the letter is being sent is a man or a woman, the salutation 'Dear Sir/Madam' can be used.

If you know the name of the person you are writing to, you can address the person by his or name accompanied by a title, as in, 'Dear Ms Uma Verma' or 'Dear Dr James'.

The subject

This part is a feature of all kinds of official letters. It is a brief statement of the subject of the letter, or what it is about and it is placed below the salutation.

The body of the letter

This is the main part of any letter. The contents of an official letter should be brief, clear, precise and complete with respect to the information being conveyed. What is just as important is that your letter must be polite, even when refusing an offer or saying something difficult for the receiver to accept. Although official letters are written in a formal style, it is best to avoid using fixed expressions such as, 'Yours of even date to hand.'

The complimentary close

The expression usually used to close official letters that begin with the salutation 'Dear sir' (and others of the same kind) is 'Yours faithfully'. But in cases where the receiver is addressed by his/her title and name, the complimentary close used is 'Yours sincerely'. Note that forms like 'Yours respectfully', 'Yours obediently' and 'Your obedient servant' are now considered old-fashioned.

The signature

Official letters must have the full signature, with the person's name and designation in two separate lines below it. If the name of the company is mentioned, it appears above the signature of its representative who writes the letter. If an employee signs a letter on behalf of a senior colleague, the name and designation of the person is given below the signature and name of the person signing the letter.

In addition to these eight parts, some official letters have all or some of the following.

Reference numbers

Official letters sent from organisations are assigned numbers that help in having the letters filed according to their subject. The reference number is placed above the sender's address in the block format.

The attention line

This sometimes appears above the salutation. It contains the name of the person to whom the letter is to be directed, especially in large organisations.

Enclosures

This is placed on the left-hand margin, below the signature line. You can list in this part of the official letter the papers you may want to enclose. For example:

encl. 1. budget for 2006–2007
      2. auditor's report

Copies

If copies of the letter are going to other persons, their names are mentioned below the list of enclosures.

Initials

The last part of an official consists of the initials of the person who dictates the letter and that of the person who types it.

Samples of official letters

1. Letter to a bank manager about change in address

129 Neeti Apartments
Kasturba Nagar
Ahmedabad 700 007
Tel. No. 26537390

5 May 2006

The Branch Manager
Bank of Baroda
25 Divya Circle
Ahmedabad 700 004

Dear Madam,

Subject: Change of address

This is with reference to my Savings Account No. 235479 at the Divya CIrcle branch. I would like to inform you that I have recently moved from 61/7 Vilas Enclave to the above address at Kasturba Nagar. I request that the change in my address and telephone number be noted and that the records be modified accordingly.

Thank you.
Yours faithfully,

Sowmya Sagar
(Sowmya Sagar)

2. Letter to a senior colleague, applying for leave

100 Park View
Kanchan Nagar
Nagpur 400 005

31 October 2006

Mr Rakesh Makhija
Combo Technologies
Nagpur

Dear Mr Makhija,

Subject: Leave application

This is to inform you that I am unwell and will not be able to attend office for two days. I would be grateful if you could grant me leave for the two days, 31 October and 1 November 2006.

Yours sincerely,

R. Vijay Rao

(R. Vijay Rao)

3. Letter written to make a business enquiry

Vidya Book House
136 Sheshagiri Colony
Adyar
Chennai 400 008

9 February 2006

The Sales Manager
Happy Hours Publishing House
67/6 Ambedkar Nagar
Mumbai 200 078

Dear Sir/Madam,

Subject: Enquiry on children's titles

We are one of the best-known booksellers in Chennai, with five outlets in different parts of the city. At present, we are in the process of building up an excellent selection of children's literature and are writing to publishers of books for children who could help us offer a huge variety to our young customers.

As a leading publishing company specialising in books for children, we are sure you would have several titles in which we would certainly be interested. We would be grateful if you could ask your sales executive in Chennai to visit us to discuss possibilities of a business relationship between our two companies. Could you also have a catalogue of your publications sent to us, please.

We look forward to hearing from you.

Yours faithfully,
for Vidya Book House

T. Sebastin

(T. Sebastin)
Manager

4. *Letter written from one branch office to another regarding internal matter*

Amravati Builders
Head Office
14 S. P. Road
Bhopal 200 008

29 March 2006

Ms Nirmala John
Amravati Builders
Regional Office
Plot No. 11 Keshavpuri
Indore 260 009

Dear Ms John,

Subject: Budget for 2006–2007

As directed by the Managing Director, Mr Prem Khosla, I am enclosing the papers related to the budget that has been finalised for the financial year 2006–2007. This is for your reference and necessary action.

With regards,

Yours sincerely,

Vikram Puri
(Vikram Puri)
for Shekhar Munim
Accounts Officer

encl. 1
copy to: Mr Prem Khosla, Managing Director, Bhopal (for information)
copy to: Mr Prasad Nambiar, Regional Manager, Indore (for information)
SM/VR

5. Letter written to make a hotel room reservation

Flat No. 6 Alpine Apartments
15/3 M G Road
Bangalore 560 002
Email: philiposej@rediffmail.com
Tel. No. (080) 26609853

24 June 2006

The Manager (Reservations)
Hotel Sea View
Beach Road
Puri 400 001

Dear Sir/Madam,

Subject: Request for reservation

I plan to be in Puri with my family from 3–6 July 2006, and we would like to stay at your hotel. I would be grateful if you could make a reservation for an air-conditioned double room with an extra bed.

I will be checking in at the hotel on the morning of 3 July and will be leaving on the afternoon of 6 July. All hotel charges will be paid at the time of check out. Could you send your confirmation by email to the above id, please.

Yours faithfully,

Philipose John Thottathil

(Philipose John Thottathil)

6. Letter written to invite an eminent person to deliver a talk

Department of Archaeology
Postgraduate College of Arts and Science
Allahabad

24 August 2006

Professor Indu Iyengar
Department of Archaeology
Delhi University

Dear Dr Iyengar,

I have great pleasure in inviting you to deliver the keynote address at the 15th National Conference on Archaeology that is scheduled to be held from 4–6 December at the Vigyan Bhavan. We expect about a hundred delegates from India and fifty delegates from abroad to attend the conference.

I would be grateful if you could confirm your acceptance of the invitation as early as possible. We will wait to hear from you before finalising the programme.

With regards,

Yours sincerely,

K. Satish Jain
Professor K. Satish Jain
Head, Department of Archaeology
Delhi University

7. A letter to the editor

4, BHEL Colony
Fire Station Lane
Belgaum
19 April 2006

The Editor
Southern Star
Chennai

Sir,

This is with reference to the report published in your newspaper on 18 April 2006 on the death of a seven-year-old boy who fell into an open manhole. I am writing to express my sense of outrage at the extreme carelessness of the municipal authorities. This is certainly not the first incident of its kind, and it is shocking that we never seem to be able to learn from our mistakes, even when many lives have already been lost. The taxes that the people of the country pay the government should certainly be enough to cover the cost of lids for manhole covers, an absolute necessity for our safety. How many more lives will need to be lost before the administration wakes up to the seriousness of the matter!

Yours truly,

Jaswant Nath
(Jaswant Nath)

8. Letter of complaint to be lodged with the police

A 31 Kamala Nagar
Bhubaneswar 546 007

1 November 2006

The SHO
Police Station
Kamala Nagar 546 007

Dear Sir,

I wish to lodge a complaint with you about the increasing incidence of thefts in the locality. Block A, where I live, is as you are aware at the far end of the colony. The street has only one light, and that has not been working for about a month now. The night watchman appointed by the residents association does not turn up for duty at least twice or thrice in a week. Over the last five months, there have been six cases of thefts, where residents here have lost cash, household goods, jewellery and expensive clothes.

We request you to investigate the matter and take necessary action to prevent such incidents in the future.

Yours faithfully,

Sally Mathias
(Sally Mathias)

9. Letter of resignation

356, Shalimar Gardens
Patna 800 002

1 August 2006

The Nursing Superintendent
Medical College Hospital
G. M. Road
Patna 800 004

Dear Madam,

Subject: Resignation

This is to inform you that I will be unable to continue working at the hospital as my family is relocating to Guwahati. I therefore resign my post of OT Nurse, Grade II, with effect from 31 October 2006, and am giving you the required 3-month notice. I would be grateful if you could relieve me on 31 October and also forward your consent to the concerned departments for the final settlement of my dues at the earliest.

I take this opportunity to thank you for the encouragement and the support that I have always received from you and also from the management as well as from my colleagues in the hospital. Being here has been both an enjoyable and a professionally satisfying experience.

With regards,

Yours faithfully,

Nafisa Dharmaraj
(Nafisa Dharmaraj)

10. Letter written to apply for a job

Flat No. 36
C Wing
Sea Breeze Apartments
Beach Road
Goa 346 087

18 November 2006

The Personnel Manager
Hotel Malabar Palace
M. G. Road
Kochi 643 008

Dear Sir/Madam,

Subject: Application for the post of Assistant Manager, Reservations

This is with reference to your advertisement in the Hindu dated 16 November 2006 calling for applications for the above post in your hotel.

I am 26 years old and I am a graduate in hotel management from the College of Vocational Studies, Mumbai. Although I belong to Madhya Pradesh, I am working at present in Hotel Surya, a three-star hotel in Goa, as a sales executive in Reservations. One of my main duties here is to liaise with travel agents and private companies and get business for the hotel. I have been with Hotel Surya since September 2003.

I enclose copies of my school and college certificates as well as a testimonial from the Manager, Reservations at Hotel Surya.

I would be grateful if you could consider me for the advertised position.

Yours faithfully,

Asif Ahmed
(Asif Ahmed)

encl. 1. copies of certificates
      2. testimonial

Letters of application can also be shorter than the above sample. This happens when the letter a encloses curriculum vitae (CV), which is also known as a résumé (pronounced re-zyu-may) in American English. The CV is an outline of your personal details, educational qualifications, work experience, languages spoken and other interests. You could also give the names of one or two referees who would be willing to testify to your character and abilities. The information should be presented in a clear, easy-to-read format. For a sample, you can look at the résumé below.

Résumé

Name	: Gagan Kapoor
Address	: B5/34 Park Lane Defence Colony Ranchi 600 006
Telephone	: 25623271
Nationality	: Indian
Date of birth	: 6 August 1970
Academic qualifications	:
• 1993	Diploma in Mechanical Engineering with 58% marks from the Government College of Engineering, Ranchi
• 1990	Passed the Senior Secondary School examination from Kendriya Vidyalaya, S. P. Chowk, Ranchi, with 75% marks
• 1988	Passed the Secondary examination from Gyan Bharat High School, Ranchi, with 60% marks
Other qualifications	: Diploma in computer applications

Work experience

June 1997–February 1998: Working as a technician in R. M. Industries, Panipet

Job profile : Communicating technical information from engineers to workers; guiding work on complex technical projects

February 1994–May 1997: Worked as a technical assistant at Prabhat Engineering Company

Job profile : Assisted in repair of industrial machinery and performed routine technical work involving application of theory

E-MAIL LETTERS

Note the structure of an e-mail letter, which has the following components.

From. The sender of the message will type his or her e-mail address here.

To. Here you can type the e-mail address of the recipient; more than one address can be written, separated by commas.

Cc (carbon copy, or copy to). Here you type a list of addresses to which you want to send copies of your message.

Bcc (blind carbon copy). The recipients' addresses, which you type here, will not be seen by other recipients. Use this if the addressee likes to keep his or her privacy.

Subject. Here you type the subject of the message. Don't leave this blank; give a specific title that will help the recipient to know what the message is about.

Attachments. These are files which go with your message. The recipient has to download them in order to read or see them.

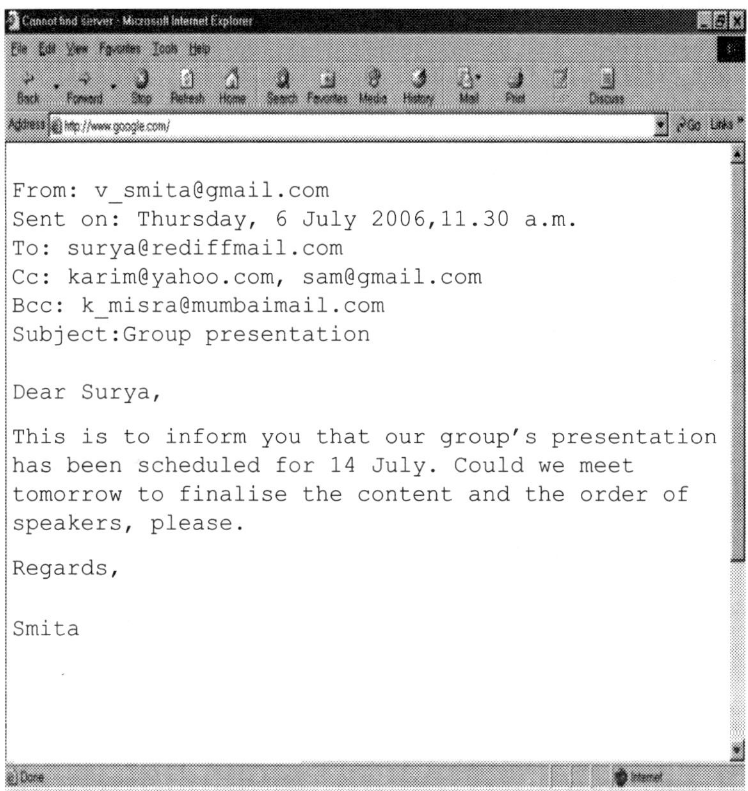
From: v_smita@gmail.com
Sent on: Thursday, 6 July 2006,11.30 a.m.
To: surya@rediffmail.com
Cc: karim@yahoo.com, sam@gmail.com
Bcc: k_misra@mumbaimail.com
Subject:Group presentation

Dear Surya,

This is to inform you that our group's presentation has been scheduled for 14 July. Could we meet tomorrow to finalise the content and the order of speakers, please.

Regards,

Smita

Exercise

1. Imagine that you are Shailendra Singh Rathore and you have just relocated to Ranchi. Write a letter to the General Manager, Bharat Sanchar Nigam Limited, R. P. Road, Ranchi 380 006, applying for a telephone connection.
2. You are Wilson Thomas, the sports captain of your college. Write a letter to Ashoka Sports Store, M. G. Road, Kochi, placing an order for a list of sports items and asking for a discount on the catalogue price.
3. As Usha Rajmohan, write a letter to the principal of your college requesting him/her to allow you five days leave. Remember to mention clearly the dates on which you need leave and your reasons for wanting it.

4. Imagine that the manager of the State Dairy Farm near your town has invited your class to visit its milk chilling and packaging plant. As Nitya Balan, class representative, write a letter thanking him for the invitation, and giving him the date and time when your class would like to make the visit and the number of students in the group.

5. As Shaila Kumar, secretary of the English literary society in your club, write a letter to a well-known Indian writer who writes in English, inviting him/her to be the chief guest on the occasion of the society's annual event, From Daffodils to Champas.

6. Imagine that you are a young parent who is disturbed at the way toddlers are burdened with examinations and homework. Write a letter to the editor of a local daily, expressing your concern.

7. You are Salim Ali of Cuttack. In response to a newspaper advertisement, write a letter to the personnel manager of Orissa Engineering Pvt Ltd, applying for the post of an assistant engineer in the company. Also prepare a CV to be enclosed in your letter.

8. You are Dr Manju Pillai of Kollam. The modem you bought two weeks ago is giving you problems. Write a letter to the manager of Asia Electronics from whom you bought the computer, making a complaint about the defective modem and asking for it to be replaced at the earliest.

9. As V. Arvind, write a letter to the general manager of the Kerala State Road Transport Corporation making a request for more college specials, which would cover different parts of your city.

10. You are Madhu Agarwal of Delhi. You have recently moved into a new house in the city. Write a letter to the postmaster of your local post office informing him/her of the change of address and requesting that your mails be redirected to your new address.

11. The *New Observer,* a newspaper, has invited readers to send letters to the editor to the e-mail address, letters@newobserver.com. Write an e-mail letter saying that their report on a seminar held in your town was misleading. The report had said that the seminar ended in confusion and disorderly behaviour by two groups of participants, which is not true.

12. You have to go to Singapore to work on a software project for your company in Bangalore. Send an e-mail message to Sandeep Travels (address: sandeep tours@sandeep.com), asking them to make travel arrangements for you to go to Singapore by air and return after a week. Specify the airline you would prefer to travel by, the dates, the class by which you want to travel, the mode of payment, the delivery instructions and your food preferences in an attachment called 'Travel details'.

5 Spoken Communication

The sounds of English come together to form words, and words are combined to form meaningful sentences that convey a complete thought—by making statements, asking questions, expressing wonder, joy, sadness or disgust. However, language is also used to perform several communicative functions. Thus, we use language to ask for directions, make a request, apologise or congratulate someone. Proficiency in performing these language functions in English is a very important part of learning to speak the language.

In this short chapter we will look at samples of some common functions in English and the language used to perform them. You can practise the expressions both alone and with your classmates in order to be able to use them with skill and confidence when speaking English.

Greeting and Taking Leave

Read the two dialogues below. Pay attention to the expressions used in situations where people greet and take leave of one another. The first dialogue occurs in a formal situation while the second one is informal.

Dialogue (formal)

(Mr Anand meets Amita, a student who lives in his neighbourhood, at a bookstore. They have met before, but do not know each other very well.)

Amita : Good morning, Mr Anand. How're you?

Mr Anand : Good morning, Amita. I'm very well, thank you. What about you?

Amita : I'm fine, thanks. We haven't met for quite sometime, have we?

Mr Anand : Yes, you're right. I have been away in Nagpur. Have you found something interesting to buy?

Amita : No, not really. I just came in a fcw minutes ago.

Mr Anand : Well, it was nice meeting you, Amita. I could have given you a lift home but I'm afraid I have to rush to keep an appointment. I do hope you'll excuse me.

Amita : Oh, that's quite all right, Mr Anand. I hope we can meet again soon.

Mr Anand : Yes, please do come over sometime. Bye!

Amita : Bye, bye, Mr Anand!

Dialogue (informal)

(Barkha meets Farha, who used to be a classmate at school, after a long time at a wedding.)

Barkha : Hello, Farha! What a lovely surprise! Good to see you after so long.

Farha : Hi, Barkha! Yes, it's great to see you too! How're you and where have you been?

Barkha : Just fine, thanks. I was away in Aligarh. And how are things with you?

Farha : Everything's okay, thanks. Hey, we must meet and catch up on all that's been happening.

Barkha : We must do that. Let me jot down your telephone number.

Farha : Here, I'll write it down for you. Wish I could have stayed longer, but I must run. Have to pick up mother from the station.

Barkha : Sure, see you sometime. Bye!

Farha : Bye, bye!

Exercise 1

Look at some expressions used to greet people and take leave of them. Read each item and repeat it. Note the use of contracted forms such as 'I'm' for 'I am' and 'you'll' for 'you will'.

- Good morning, how are you?
- I'm very well, thank you. What about you?
- I'm fine, thanks.
- We haven't met for quite sometime, have we?
- It's a pleasure to see you.
- It was nice meeting you, but I'm afraid I have to go now.
- I must leave. I hope you'll excuse me.
- That's quite all right. I hope we can meet again soon.
- Yes, we must.
- Yes, I hope so too.
- Yes, please do come over.
- Bye, bye!

Exercise 2

Look at some other more informal expressions used to greet people and take leave of them. Read each item and repeat it as you did in Exercise 1.

- Hello! What a lovely surprise!
- Good to see you after so long.
- Hi! Its great to see you too.
- How're you and where have you been?
- Just fine, thanks. How're things with you?
- Everything's okay, thanks.
- We must meet and catch up on what's happening.
- Yes, we must do that.
- Wish I could have stayed longer, but I must run.
- Sure, see you sometime. Bye, bye!

Exercise 3

Working in pairs, write and enact the following situations in the form of brief dialogues choosing appropriate expressions from those given above.

1. Nita is on her way to her violin class. She meets Dr Prakash, her father's boss, outside the music school. The two persons greet each other and exchange a few words before taking leave.
2. Abhay runs into Abdul, a friend, at a supermarket. The two men greet each other and exchange a few words before taking leave.

Introducing Yourself

Read the dialogue below. Pay attention to the expressions used in situations where people introduce themselves to each other in a formal situation. Note that the same expressions can be used in an informal situation as well except for those used to greet and take leave of each other (refer to the function above).

Dialogue (formal)

(Mrs Shakti Thomas walks up to Mr Abhay Sarkar, an employee in the bank where she has just started work.)

Mrs Thomas : Good morning! I'm Shakti Thomas. I've joined the bank today as an assistant accounts officer. I was with a private finance company in Trichy earlier.

Mr Sarkar (rising to his feet): Good morning! I'm happy to meet you. I'm Abhay Sarkar, and I'm a manager in the housing loans division. Welcome to our bank!

Mrs Thomas : Thank you, Mr Sarkar. Very nice meeting you too.

Exercise

Look at some expressions used in both formal and informal situations to introduce yourself to somebody. Read each item and repeat it with a name of your choice.

1. Good morning!/Hello! My name is ....
2. Good morning!/Hi! I'm ....
3. I have just joined ....
4. I have just moved in ....
5. I'm from ....
6. I work for ....
7. I'm the new ....

Introducing People to One Another

Read the two dialogues below. Pay attention to the expressions used in situations where a person introduces people to one another. The first dialogue occurs in a formal situation while the second occurs in an informal one.

Dialogue (formal)

(Dr Preeta Rao and Mr Salil Mohammad meet for the first time at the workplace of a common friend, Mrs Padma Padamsee.)

Mrs Padamsee : Dr Rao, I'd like to introduce you to Mr Salil Mohammad. Mr Mohammad is our company secretary. Mr Mohammad, please meet Dr Preeta Rao. Dr Rao is an educational advisor with the UNICEF.

Dr Rao (shaking hands): How d'you do, Mr Mohammad? I'm happy to meet you.

Mr Mohammad : Thank you, Dr Rao. This is indeed a pleasure. Mrs Padamsee has spoken to me about the fine work that you are doing among children in government schools.

Dialogue (informal)

(Kritika introduces her sister Alka to her classmate John.)

Kritika : John, this is my sister, Alka. She's an editor with the *Times of India*. Alka, meet John. He's my classmate and captain of the college basketball team.

John : Hi, Alka! Nice meeting you.

Alka : Hello, John. It's nice meeting you too. I used to know your cousin Stella at the K. N. Degree College.

Exercise 1

Look at some expressions used in formal and in informal situations to introduce two persons to each other and those that they can use to respond. Read each item and repeat it filling in a name of your choice.

1. I'd like to introduce you to ....
2. Please meet ....
3. This is ....
4. ...., meet ....
5. I'm happy to meet you.
6. This is indeed a pleasure.
7. Nice meeting you.

Exercise 2

Working first in pairs and then in groups of three, write and enact the following situations in the form of brief dialogues choosing appropriate expressions from those given above.

1. Rohit Kumar from Alpha Electronics, Kanpur, enters the Delhi office of his company's chartered accountant with whom he has an appointment. He introduces himself to the person's secretary, explaining who he is, where he is from and why he is there.
2. Dharam goes to his friend Praveen's house. His cousin, Smita, is with him. Dharam introduces the two to each other.

Making Requests and Asking for Directions

Read the dialogues below. Pay attention to the expressions used in situations where requests are made for help and to seek directions.

Dialogue (formal)

(Vikram is filling in a form at a railway booking counter when his pen stops writing. He turns to a stranger standing next to him and requests her to lend him a pen.)

Vikram : I'm sorry to bother you, but I need your help. My pen is not writing. May I borrow yours, please?

Stranger : Certainly. Here, you can use this pen.

Vikram : (uses the pen and returns it to its owner): I've completed filling in the form. Thank you very much!

Stranger : You're welcome!

Dialogue (informal)

(Vimala asks her friend Aman if he could get an application form from the passport office.)

Vimala : Aman, could you do me a favour, please. I'd like you to pick up a passport application form for me on your way back from office.

Aman : Sure, I'll do that today.

Vimala : Hope it won't be a problem.

Aman : Of course not! No problem at all.

Vimala : Thanks!

Aman : Not at all.

Dialogue (formal)

(Lata is on her way to her friend's office and has lost her way. She stops a passerby and asks for directions.)

Lata : Excuse me, please. Could you tell me how to get to Kedarpuri junction, please.

Passerby : Certainly, just go straight ahead and then take the second turning to your left. Drive on until you see a children's park. Turn right and then right again and you'll find yourself at the Kedarpuri junction. Have you understood?

Lata : Yes, that shouldn't be difficult to find. Thank you very much.

Passerby : You're welcome.

Exercise 1

Look at some expressions used in both formal and informal situations to make requests and also to respond to them. Read each item and repeat it, using the right intonation.

- Do you think I could use your telephone, please?
- Could I ask a favour of you?
- Excuse me, could you help me, please.
- I'm sorry to trouble you, but I need your help.
- Would you mind helping me with this, please?
- I wonder if you could do me a favour.
- Certainly, I shall be glad to help.
- Sure. I'd be glad to help.
- Of course, by all means.
- Thank you.
- Thank you very much.
- Thanks a lot.
- You're most welcome.
- You're welcome.
- Not at all.

Exercise 2

Working in pairs, write and enact the following situations in the form of brief dialogues choosing appropriate expressions from those given above.

1. Mr Joseph has just arrived in Guntur and asks a traffic policeman for directions to a hotel where his office has made arrangements for his stay.

2. Chandra requests her neighbour, Madhu, to teach her to bake a cake.
3. Priya goes to the head of her department with a request for a day's leave.

Making and Accepting an Apology

Read the dialogues below. Pay attention to the expressions used in situations where an apology is called for. Also note how an apology is accepted.

Dialogue (formal)

(Asif Abdullah supplies material for a construction company. There is a delay in the delivery of a truckload of steel because of which the company had to lose three valuable days of work besides wages paid to the workers. Asif apologises to the managing director of the company.)

Asif : Ms Bharadwaj, I must apologise for the delay in the delivery of the steel you had ordered. I fully understand the loss it must have meant to you. It all happened because of the transport strike and I was really helpless in the matter. I'm sincerely sorry and hope you'll excuse the delay.

Ms Bharadwaj : Mr Abdullah, you're right about the loss that the delay on your part caused us. We don't blame you fully for we do know that it was caused by the strike. We'll accept your apologies and hope that this kind of a thing does not happen again.

Asif : Thank you for being so understanding, Ms Bharadwaj.

Dialogue (informal)

(Jeevan knocks over a crystal vase, breaking it into pieces. His mother scolds him, and he apologises to her.)

Mother : Jeevan, you've broken my favourite vase! How can you be so careless!

Jeevan : Ma, I'm so sorry. I was running to answer the telephone and slipped on the freshly mopped floor. Please forgive me.

Mother : All right, but do be a little careful in future when you go about the house.

Jeevan : Thanks, Ma! I promise that I won't run about inside the house again.

Exercise 1

Look at some expressions used in both formal and informal situations to make apologies and also to respond to them. Read each item and repeat it, using the right intonation.

- I must apologise for…
- I'm terribly sorry about…
- Please accept my sincere apologies.
- I hope you'll excuse me.
- Please forgive me.
- I'm so sorry.
- It won't happen again, I promise.
- I'm really ashamed of myself.
- It's quite all right.
- I really hope it won't happen again.
- No need to feel so bad about it. These things happen.

Exercise 2

Working in pairs, write and enact the following situations in the form of brief dialogues choosing appropriate expressions from those given above.

1. Parveen forgets to wish her friend Anju on her birthday and calls her to apologise. Anju assures her that it is all right.
2. Ashok Garg apologises to his senior colleague, Tony Alfred, for a mistake that he made in drafting a legal document. Alfred excuses Ashok.

Inviting and Accepting/Declining an Invitation

Read the dialogues below. Pay attention to the expressions used in situations where an invitation is extended and it is accepted or declined.

Dialogue (formal)

(Mr Gopal Reddy invites two colleagues to his son's engagement dinner.)

Reddy : Good morning, Rita! Good morning, Mrs Iyer! There's some happy news I must tell you about.

Rita : We're so happy for you, Mr Reddy.

Mrs Iyer : Do tell us what it is, Mr Reddy.

Reddy : My son, Rahul, is getting engaged on the twenty-fifth of this month. My wife and I will be happy if you both along with your families could come to the engagement that will be followed by a dinner at the YWCA convention centre at seven in the evening.

Rita : Congratulations, Mr Reddy, and thanks for the invitation. I'll certainly be there with my family.

Reddy : Thank you very much, Rita. We look forward to seeing you.

Mrs Iyer : Congratulations, Mr Reddy. Thank you for inviting us. I wish we could have come, but I'm sorry we'll have to miss the engagement. I'm leaving on the twenty-second for Bangalore with my family. What a pity!

Reddy : Yes, it's so disappointing that you won't be able to attend the function. We'll all miss you. However, please don't worry, Mrs Iyer. I understand.

Dialogue (informal)

(Rema sees her friends Usha and Teja in the colony park and goes up to speak to them.)

Rema : Hello, Usha! Hi, Teja!

Usha and Teja (together): Hi, Rema!

Rema : I was planning to call and speak to you both. I'm having a small party on Friday evening at five o'clock. Why don't you both come?

Usha : Sure, I'd love to! I'll be there early to help you put finishing touches to everything.

Rema : Thanks, Usha. It'll be nice having you at the party.

Teja : The party's on Friday, isn't it? I'm sorry but I don't think I'll be able to make it. You see, my mother is getting operated for gall bladder stones on Thursday. I'll need to be with her in the hospital. Thanks for asking me.

Rema : You're welcome, Teja. Everyone's going to miss your music at the party. But we'll make it up some other time.

Exercise 1

Look at some expressions used in both formal and informal situations to extend invitations and also to accept and decline them. Read each item and repeat it, using the right intonation.

- There's some good news.
- I'm so happy to hear that.
- My son is getting engaged.
- I'll be happy if you and your family could come.
- Are you free tomorrow evening?
- Why don't you join us at a get-together?
- Thank you for the invitation. We'll certainly come.
- It'll be a pleasure.
- Oh, sure. I'd love to come!
- Thank you for inviting me. I wish I could have come.
- I'm afraid I'll not be able to come.
- I'm sorry, but I'll have to miss the engagement.

- What a pity you won't be able to come!
- Thank you so much. We look forward to seeing you.
- Thanks for saying yes. Be there on time.
- It's disappointing that you won't be there.
- We'll all miss you.
- It can't be helped, I suppose. But we'll make it up some other time.

Exercise 2

Working in groups of three, write and enact the following situations in the form of brief dialogues choosing appropriate expressions from those given above.

1. The general manager of a company invites two colleagues to lunch. One accepts and the other declines the invitation because of some other engagement.
2. Anita invites her friends, Hari and Rina, to go with her family on a picnic. Rina accepts the invitation but Hari declines it because of urgent work that he has to attend to on that day.

Making a Complaint

Read the dialogues below. Pay attention to the expressions used in situations, social and business, where a complaint is made.

Dialogue (formal)

(Mrs Nair goes to her neighbour, Shamim, to make a complaint.)

Mrs Nair : Good evening, Mr Shamim. I'm sorry to trouble you, but there's a small problem that I want to speak to you about.

Shamim : What is it, Mrs Nair?

Mrs Nair : There seems to be a leak in your bathroom pipe and the water seeps through the roof of our flat downstairs. Could you have the pipe repaired, please.

Shamim : Oh, I'm terribly sorry. I knew the pipe had a leak

somewhere, but I didn't realise that it was causing damage to your flat. Please forgive me. I'll have the pipe repaired immediately.

Mrs Nair : That's very kind of you, Mr Shamim. I hope you didn't mind my bringing up this matter.

Shamim : Oh no, Mrs Nair. I'm glad you brought the problem to my notice. I wouldn't have known about it otherwise.

Dialogue (formal)

(The new washing machine that Shashi Bajaj bought stops working after being used for just two days. In spite of the calls she makes, the dealer does not send a service engineer to take a look at it. Shashi goes to the company's office to make a complaint to the manager in charge of the customer service division.)

Shashi : Good morning, Mr Dutta. I have a complaint to make.

Dutta : Good morning, ma'am. Could you tell me what the problem is, please.

Shashi : I bought a Fine Wash fully automatic washing machine from Mayuri, your dealer at Prabhat Nagar, on the 12th of this month. The machine was installed on the 13th. It ran well for two days but on the third day, it simply stopped working. Mayuri has not responded to any of my calls. I'd like you to help me in getting the piece replaced.

Dutta : This is most unfortunate, ma'am. I assure you that the defective machine will be replaced by a fresh piece before evening. Please accept my apologies.

Shashi : Thank you, Mr Dutta, for being so understanding and helpful. I'm sorry for having bothered you.

Dialogue (informal)

(Anil and Afifa are close friends. Anil gets selected to the IPS but forgets to tell Afifa about it. Afifa is hurt and complains to Anil about his behaviour.)

Afifa : Anil, I'm very upset with you.

Anil : Why, Afifa, what have I done?

Afifa : I hear that you have been selected to the Indian Police Service. I'm surprised that you didn't think of telling me about it.

Anil : Oh Afifa, I'm so very sorry! I don't know why I thought that you were with all our other friends when I broke the news. Do forgive me if you can.

Afifa : That's all right. These things happen sometimes. I knew you wouldn't deliberately do a thing like that.

Exercise 1

Look at some expressions used in both formal and informal situations to make complaints. Read each item and repeat it, using the right intonation.

- I'm sorry to trouble you, but there's a problem I'd like to speak to you about.
- It would help if you could have the leaking pipe repaired.
- That's very kind of you.
- I hope you didn't mind.
- I have a complaint to make.
- My new washing machine is not working.
- Your dealer has not responded to my calls.
- I'd like to have the piece replaced.
- I insist on having the piece replaced.
- Thank you for being so understanding and helpful.
- I'm sorry to have bothered you.
- I'm very upset with you.
- I'm very annoyed with you.
- I'm surprised you didn't think of giving me the good news.
- That's all right.
- I guess these things happen.
- Let's just forget it, shall we?

Exercise 2

Working in pairs, write and enact the following situations in the form of brief dialogues choosing appropriate expressions from those given above.

1. Mr Nigam has by mistake been sent a huge bill by the telephone department for calls made on another number. He goes to meet the official in charge of billing at the Bharat Sanchar Nigam office in his area and make a formal complaint.
2. Maria finds that her sister has forgotten to feed the parrot that she left in her care while out of station. She calls her on the telephone and complains.

Congratulating, Expressing Sympathy and Offering Condolences

Read the dialogues below. Pay attention to the expressions used in situations that call for congratulating, expressing sympathy and offering condolences.

Dialogue

(Satish's essay on conservation of natural resources wins the first prize in an international competition organised by the UNESCO. His thesis supervisor, Dr Neeru Das, congratulates Satish on his achievement.)

Dr Neeru Das : Satish, I just heard the wonderful news. Congratulations on your remarkable achievement.

Satish : Thank you very much, Dr Das. It is all because of the encouragement and help that I have always got from you.

Dr Neeru Das : Not entirely. It's a result of your own hard work and perseverance. Satish, you really deserve this honour. Everyone in the department is really proud of you. I'm sure you will keep up the good work.

Satish : Thank you, ma'am. It's very kind of you.

Dialogue

(Sudha does not make it to the university basketball team in spite of the months of hard work she has put in. Her coach, Abraham, expresses his sympathy and consoles Sudha.)

Abraham : Sudha, I'm sorry about your not getting selected for the university basketball team. I can understand just how you feel after all the hard work you put in.

Sudha : Sir, this is really terribly disappointing! I don't know where I went wrong.

Abraham : Look Sudha, you mustn't let yourself be disheartened by this small setback. I just know how good you are. If it will make you feel better, the selectors had a very difficult time in coming to a final decision on the team. You must realise that these things are all a part of the game and must sportingly accept what has happened.

Dialogue

(Tanya has lost her grandfather. Her friend, Meher, comes to offer his condolences.)

Meher : Tanya, I'm truly sorry about your grandfather. I understand how shattered you feel at the moment.

Tanya : I can't believe he is gone forever. I'll always miss him so badly.

Meher : Yes, Tanya, your grandfather was indeed a special person. Nobody who met him could fail to adore him. It is a great loss, but we must be grateful for the fact that he went peacefully in his sleep without the least suffering.

Tanya : Thank you, Meher. I don't know how I could have coped without all of you.

Exercise 1

Look at some expressions used in both formal and informal situations to congratulate somebody on an achievement, to express sympathy and to offer condolences. Read each item and repeat it, using the right intonation. Remember that these are situations that call for sincerity and genuine feeling and in the absence of these, the words become mere clichés.

- Congratulations!
- We are proud of you.
- You really deserve this honour.
- Very well done! Keep it up!
- I'm sure this won't happen again.
- I've no doubt that you'll do much better next time.
- I just got the sad news. This must be a terrible blow to all of you.
- It is a great loss indeed.
- You must be brave.
- Remember that we are all with you.
- I'm sorry about what happened.
- You mustn't let this depress you.

Exercise 2

Working in pairs, write and enact the following situations in the form of brief dialogues choosing appropriate expressions from those given above.

1. Prabha is in bed with jaundice. She will not be able to take the final examinations in two subjects. Her aunt visits her to express sympathy and comfort her.
2. Professor Prasad has won ICAR's Scientist of the Year Award. His colleague Dr Susie Sapra congratulates him.
3. On hearing about the death of Steve's mother, Rajesh visits his colleague to offer his condolences.

Making Suggestions, Offering Advice and Persuading

Read the dialogues below. Pay attention to the expressions used in situations that call for making a suggestion, offering advice and persuading.

Dialogue

(Kamala drops in at the local youth club to watch a group of young people rehearse for a play they plan to put up shortly.)

Kamala : That was very entertaining. I enjoyed every minute of the play.

Maya : Thank you, Kamala, for sitting through our rehearsal.

Nasir : Any suggestions, Kamala? We have been at this for so long and have stopped seeing things clearly.

Kamala : Well, first I suggest that you could think of another title for the play. I don't think the present title is either interesting or suitable.

Maya : That's a good suggestion. What's your second suggestion, Kamala?

Kamala : In my opinion, Maya, the character of the old woman whom you play could appear at the end of the play to say why she behaved as she did. Do you think it will be possible?

Nasir : Why not? We'll try that one out. Anything else, Kamala?

Kamala : No, that's all. I really feel you have a wonderful play there.

Maya : Thanks a lot, Kamala! You have been of great help.

Dialogue

(Mrs Leela Pai finds her neighbour Ms Preet Hemchandani anxious about her father's illness.)

Mrs Pai : Hello, Preet! Why do you look so anxious?

Preet : Hello, Mrs Pai. Do come in. I'm very worried about father's fever. It just doesn't seem to be coming down. The doctor is not available on Sundays. I don't know what to do.

Mrs Pai : Look Preet, let me offer you some advice. There is no need to worry yourself sick. Your father is on antibiotics, and the infection will come under control in a day or two. Meanwhile, you could try applying a cold compress on his forehead. You must remove that thick blanket and cover him with a light cotton sheet instead. Also, remember that it is important for him to have as much fluids as you can possibly get inside him. However, don't give him anything too cold. Sit by his side for at least a few minutes whenever you can and, please, do appear cheerful. Don't you worry, Preet. Mr Hemchandani is going to be his old self in another three or four days. As for now, please don't hesitate to call me if you feel you need my help.

Dialogue

(Mallika is going to move to a suburb, away from the noise and pollution of the city where she has lived for many years. She tries to persuade her friend, Farida, to do so too.)

Mallika : Farida, did I tell you that I am moving soon to Green Park colony, which is about 20 km from the city?

Farida : Oh! That's so far!

Mallika : You are mistaken, Farida. It's not really as far as you think it is. In fact, why don't you consider moving there yourself?

Farida : Well, I really don't think I would like the idea of staying so far from the city.

Mallika : Look, Farida, could I persuade you to go along with me and see the place for yourself? It's just a fifteen-minute drive from here. The road to the place is wide and open, with hardly any traffic. There are shops, schools, a bank, a post office and two nursing homes around the colony. Besides the greenery is amazing! I'm sure you'll decide to move there as soon as you set eyes on the place. Why don't you have a look at the colony?

Farida : All right, Mallika, I'll go with you today. You really know the art of persuading people, don't you?

Exercise 1

Look at some expressions used in both formal and informal situations to offer suggestions, to advise or to persuade. Read each item and repeat it, using the right intonation.

- I suggest you repeat these expressions twice each.
- I think you should repeat these expressions as often as you can.
- Let's repeat these expressions for practice.
- Why don't we repeat these expressions a few more times?
- I really advise you to repeat these expressions several times.
- You should repeat these expressions in order to perfect them.
- They ought to repeat these expressions if they wish to speak fluently.
- Why don't you try repeating these expressions?
- Do try repeating these expressions.
- Could I persuade you to repeat these expressions as many times as possible?

Exercise 2

Working in pairs, write and enact the following situations in the form of brief dialogues choosing appropriate expressions from those given above.

1. Madhuri finds her brother, Manu slipping in his studies. She advises him on how he could pull himself up again.
2. Bhatia gives suggestions to his junior colleagues on how to promote a new brand of health drink.
3. Manohar persuades his friends to visit an exhibition of Indian art.

Expressing Agreement/Disagreement and Seeking Clarification

Read the dialogues below. Pay attention to the expressions used in situations that call for polite forms of expressing agreement and disagreement and also for interrupting a speaker to seek some clarification.

Dialogue

(Anju, Jessie and Siddique are discussing the idea of a cultural show they plan to organise for an orphanage where Anju's mother is a committee member.)

Anju : I'm glad you both agreed to help me organise a cultural show for 'Aashraya'. My mother is very happy at the thought of the children having a wonderful evening.

Jessie : It's a pleasure, Anju. I'm sure we can put together something exciting that will keep the young ones glued to their seats.

Siddique : The next step is to think of what kind of programme we should have. I think we could have a play in Hindi done by a good theatre group.

Anju : Yes, I quite agree with you. That would interest the children. Besides, it would be an opportunity to introduce them to the delights of theatre.

Jessie : I'm sorry, but I'll differ on that. A long play will make the children restless and even bored.

Siddique : Perhaps you're right. Listen, since the show is going to happen a day before Deepavali, how about having a programme of Indian music and dance on a stage lit up with tiny diyas?

Anju : That sounds lovely, but I'm afraid I can't accept the idea of having diyas burning so close to the two hundred children packed into a tiny auditorium.

Jessie : You're right, Anju, we really can't take any risks. But what would you say to our having tiny electric bulbs and also to our having the programme in the open?

Anju : In that case, I think Siddique's suggestion is great.

Dialogue

(Professor Bakshi is lecturing on human evolution in his anthropology class. Adela raises her hand to get his attention.)

Dr Bakshi : . . . and so we share a common ancestor with gorillas and chimpanzees. We . . .

Adela : Excuse me, sir. I'm sorry to interrupt, but I remember reading that we are closer in terms of our genetic makeup to chimps than we are to gorillas. Is that true?

Dr Bakshi : Yes, that's absolutely right. We separated from gorillas about ten million years ago and from chimpanzees, our closest relatives, about seven million years ago.

Adela : I have another doubt, sir. Is the theory supported by genetic evidence?

Dr Bakshi : A good question! The answer to that is yes. Over 98 per cent of our DNA is the same as that of the chimpanzees and about 97.5 per cent is the same as that of the gorillas.

Adela : Thank you, sir.

Exercise 1

Look at some expressions used in both formal and informal situations to express agreement and disagreement, and to seek clarification on something. Read each item and repeat it, using the right intonation.

- I quite agree with you.
- Perhaps you're right.
- I'm afraid, I'll differ with you on that point.
- I'm sorry, but I can't agree with you there.
- I'm afraid, I can't accept the idea.
- You're absolutely right.
- Excuse me. I'm sorry to interrupt, but I have a doubt that I'd like you to clarify.
- Pardon me for interrupting, but is it true that ....?

Exercise 2

Working in pairs, write and enact the following situations in the form of brief dialogues choosing appropriate expressions from those given above.

a. Two persons discuss the issue of euthanasia. They agree on some points and disagree on others.

b. Ms Anjali Majumdar is giving a talk on the first topic in your physics textbook. You have a doubt and would like Ms Majumdar to explain a point she has made before she continues her lecture. You ask for clarification politely.

Some more samples of dialogues used in different functional situations are given below for your reference and practice.

At a railway booking office

Kavya : Excuse me, ma'am, could you please tell me if there are sleeper class tickets available for Friday, 21 July on the Kerala Express to New Delhi.

Booking assistant : Sure. I'll let you know in a moment. (Checks on her computer.) I'm afraid there are no tickets available for the 21st. Could you tell me how many tickets you need?

Kavya : I need just one ticket. It's really very urgent.

Booking assistant : Oh, in that case, why don't you buy a tatkal ticket? There will be no problem at all in getting one. Please go to counter no. 6.

Kavya : Thank you very much, ma'am. You have been most helpful.

Booking assistant : You're welcome.

At a restaurant

Anthony (to a waiter) : Could we have a table for four, please We prefer one away from the entrance door.

Waiter : Certainly, sir. Will this corner table be all right?

Anthony : Thank you, this is fine. (Everyone sits down at the table.)

Waiter (after filling glasses with water and offering the menu card) : What can I get you, sir?

Anthony (after going through the card and discussing with the other people in the group) : Could you take our order, please. We will have three vegetarian thalis and one masala dosa. We would also like to have two cold coffees and two lassis. Could you repeat the order, please.

Waiter (after repeating the order) : Can I get you anything else, sir?

Anthony : Thank you, no. That will be all.

At an enquiry counter

Sujata : Good afternoon.

Person at the counter : Good afternoon, ma'am. How can I help you?

Sujata : I would like to have some information, please. Could you tell me how I could get my passport renewed, please?

Person at the counter : Certainly, ma'am. Please go up to the passport renewal section on the third floor and ask for Mr Shamim Abbas, the person looking after renewals. You can leave your application, photographs and other documents with him. Mr Abbas will also answer any queries that you may have.

Sujata : Thank you so much for guiding me.

Person at the counter : That's all right, ma'am. We're here to help.

At a shop

Shop assistant (to customer)	:	Excuse me, sir. Can I help you, please.
Customer	:	Yes, thank you. I am looking for a cotton sari for my daughter. Could you show me some, please.
Shop assistant	:	Certainly, sir. (getting a dozen saris to the counter) Here you are, sir. These are all printed cotton saris, sir. We have a wide range of prints and colours in these.
Customer	:	They are all very nice. But I think I will buy a handloom sari. Could I see some, please?
Shop assistant	:	Oh, yes, sir. (bringing another pile of saris to the counter) These are handloom saris from different parts of the country. Do you like any of them, sir?
Customer	:	This green pochampalli is beautiful. I'll take it.
Shop assistant	:	Anything else,sir?
Customer	:	No, thank you. Could I have the bill, please. Also, do you accept credit cards or will I need to pay in cash?
Shop assistant	:	A credit card will be fine, sir.
Customer	:	Thank you.
Shop assistant	:	You're most welcome,sir.

On the telephone

A: Hello, is this 26653774? My name is Rekha Jacob and I am calling from Mumbai. Could I speak to Sajid Rehman, please.

B: Could you hold the line, please. I'll see if he is in. *(after a few moments)* I'm sorry, but Mr Rehman is in a meeting. Would you like to leave a message for him?

A: Yes, please. Could you tell him that the documents he wanted have been sent by courier yesterday evening. Could you also ask him to call me back on 9846740971, please.

B : I'll give Mr Rehman your message.

A: Thank you.

B : That's all right.

Appendix 1

Correction of Common Errors

Appendix 1 is a list of some errors that Indian learners usually make when speaking and writing the language. You can use this both for easy reference and as practice material that should help you avoid making some very common mistakes. The errors relate to different areas of grammar and also to vocabulary. In the sentences listed in pairs below, the first sentence with a ✗ mark at the end is incorrect while the second one marked with a ✓ is correct. Finally, the errors in the sentences as well as their corrections have been highlighted to make you conscious of what is grammatically unacceptable in English and of what is acceptable.

1. I *have read* the book yesterday. ✗
   I *read* the book yesterday. ✓
2. They lived *at* Nellore. ✗
   They lived *in* Nellore. ✓
3. My son is going to study in *United States*. ✗
   My son is going to study in *the United States*. ✓
4. *The crocodiles* are reptiles. ✗
   Crocodiles are reptiles. ✓
5. Where *is* the scissors? ✗
   Where *are* the scissors? ✓
6. Sindhu selected the *furnitures* for her mother. ✗
   Sindhu selected the *furniture* for her mother. ✓
7. *The human beings* are polluting the environment. ✗
   Human beings are polluting the environment. ✓
8. The bowl of nuts *are* on the table. ✗
   The bowl of nuts *is* on the table. ✓
9. Could you *return back* the library cards to me, please. ✗
   Could you *return* the library cards to me, please. ✓

10. Rana has known Sumit *since* three years. ✗
Rana has known Sumit *for* three years. ✓

11. Either you or she *are* presenting a paper. ✗
Either you or she *is presenting* a paper. ✓

12. They did not see *nobody* there. ✗
They did not see *anybody* there. ✓

13. *The* oranges are rich in vitamin C. ✗
Oranges are rich in vitamin C. ✓

14. Harsha *don't* know Hindi. ✗
Harsha *doesn't* know Hindi. ✓

15. Do you have *some* books? ✗
Do you have *any* books? ✓

16. The painting is *too* beautiful. ✗
The painting is *very* beautiful. ✓

17. By the time Thomas found an umbrella, it *stopped* raining. ✗
By the time Thomas found an umbrella, it *had stopped* raining. ✓

18. I am a student here, *isn't it*? ✗
I am a student here, *aren't I*? ✓

19. They often *goes* to the city. ✗
They often *go* to the city. ✓

20. Appan is in *army*. ✗
Appan is in *the army*. ✓

21. India is playing *an* one-day cricket match against Australia. ✗
India is playing *a* one-day cricket match against Australia. ✓

22. They live very close to *Bharatapuzha* river. ✗
They live very close to *the Bharatapuzha* river. ✓

23. *The gold* is getting more and more expensive everyday. ✗
Gold is getting more and more expensive everyday. ✓

24. Rohit *has eaten* breakfast just an hour ago but he is still hungry. ✗
Rohit *ate* breakfast just an hour ago but he is still hungry. ✓

25. Mother will buy me a watch when she *will go* shopping. ✗
Mother will buy me a watch when she *goes* shopping. ✓

26. The child *is having* a hearing problem. ✗
The child *has* a hearing problem. ✓

27. This house is *more larger* that that one. ✗
This house is *larger* that that one. ✓

28. Please divide this *among* the two of you. ✗
Please divide this *between* the two of you. ✓

29. Although I was tired, *yet* I went to the party. ✗
Although I was tired, I went to the party. ✓

30. Why *you have come* so early? ✗
Why *have you come* so early? ✓

31. The doctor made him *to take* rest. ✗
The doctor made him *take* rest. ✓

32. Venu camped *besides* the lake. ✗
Venu camped *beside* the lake. ✓

33. In a corner of the room, stood a *wooden large* cupboard. ✗
In a corner of the room, stood a *large wooden* cupboard. ✓

34. The man seems *rather* healthy. ✗
The man seems *fairly* healthy. ✓

35. She hadn't done the work, *did she*? ✗
She hadn't done the work, *had she*? ✓

36. Rema gave *to me* the bracelet. ✗
Rema gave *me* the bracelet. (or Rema gave the bracelet to me.) ✓

37. If he *took* an umbrella, he would not have got drenched. ✗
If he *had taken* an umbrella, he would not have got drenched. ✓

38. Where *you are* staying? ✗
Where *are you* staying? ✓

39. *I and Suresh* went on a long trip. ✗
Suresh and I went on a long trip. ✓

40. They *doesn't* sell fresh vegetables. ✗
They *don't* sell fresh vegetables. ✓

41. The earth *is rotating* on its axis. ✗
The earth *rotates* on its axis. ✓

42. Ten thousand rupees *are* a lot of money. ✗
Ten thousand rupees *is a* lot of money. ✓
43. By the time you speak to him, he *will hear* about it. ✗
By the time you speak to him, he *will have heard* about it. ✓
44. One of the boys *have qualified* in the entrance test. ✗
One of the boys *has qualified* in the entrance test. ✓
45. *Rajans* are always ready to help with the children. ✗
The Rajans are always ready to help with the children. ✓
46. Sally avoided *to meet* people. ✗
Sally avoided *meeting* people. ✓
47. Raju went to *hospital* to get his blood pressure checked. ✗
Raju went to *the hospital* to get his blood pressure checked. ✓
48. Have you had *the breakfast*? ✗
Have you had *breakfast*? ✓
49. The boy as well as his parents *are coming* today. ✗
The boy as well as his parents *is coming* today. ✓
50. I *am hearing* music being played. ✗
I *hear* music being played. ✓
51. Azad went to the language school *for learning* Japanese. ✗
Azad went to the language school *to learn* Japanese. ✓
52. Who has left a *half-ate* guava on the table? ✗
Who has left a *half-eaten* guava on the table? ✓
53. You can write to the company for *farther* information. ✗
You can write to the company for *further* information. ✓
54. No sooner *he had* finished college than he found a job. ✗
No sooner *had he* finished college than he found a job. ✓
55. Neither Mansi nor her friends *is* in the computer lab. ✗
Neither Mansi nor her friends *are* in the computer lab. ✓
56. Have you read *Guru Granth Sahib*? ✗
Have you read *the Guru Granth Sahib*? ✓
57. The doctor and *nurse* are in the theatre. ✗
The doctor and *the nurse* are in the theatre. ✓
58. I *am thinking* that Binu will come home today. ✗
I *think* that Binu will come home today. ✓

59. She sent her son *thousand rupees.* ✗
    She sent her son *a thousand rupees.* ✓
60. Either the tourists or their guide *have talked* to the press. ✗
    Either the tourists or their guide *has talked* to the press. ✓
61. That shop stocks good *stationary.* ✗
    That shop stocks good *stationery.* ✓
62. I *am climbing* three flights of stairs every day. ✗
    I *climb* three flights of stairs every day. ✓
63. Fatima knows *to make* Tanjore paintings. ✗
    Fatima knows *how to make* Tanjore paintings. ✓
64. Please don't *repeat* the mistake *again.* ✗
    Please don't *repeat* the mistake. ✓
65. David *not only* helped his family but also everyone else in the village. ✗
    David helped *not only* his family but also everyone else in the village. ✓
66. Tell us when *will the bank* open. ✗
    Tell us when *the bank will* open. ✓
67. One cannot predict *their* own future. ✗
    One cannot predict *one's* own future. ✓
68. The volume *comprises of* twenty papers. ✗
    The volume *comprises* (or *consists of*) twenty papers. ✓
69. What is your *cousin sister* doing? ✗
    What is your *cousin* doing? ✓
70. Lekha prefers hockey *than* football. ✗
    Lekha prefers hockey *to* football. ✓
71. I saw Chinnu *a hour and a half* ago. ✗
    I saw Chinnu *an hour and a half* ago. ✓
72. Her children are very young. They are at *the school.* ✗
    Her children are very young. They still are at *school.* ✓
73. They will *either come* today or on Monday. ✗
    They will *come either* today or on Monday. ✓
74. Anu plays *violin.* ✗
    Anu plays *the violin.* ✓

75. We *did not go* to the cinema since Tony left. ✗
We *have not gone* to the cinema since Tony left. ✓

76. I need your *advise*. ✗
I need your *advice*. ✓

77. The water is *very hot* to drink. ✗
The water is *too hot* to drink. ✓

78. I *will look forward* to hearing from you. ✗
I *look forward* to hearing from you. ✓

79. The police rushed to the spot, but the burglar *already fled*. ✗
The police rushed to the spot, but the burglar *had already fled*. ✓

80. The salesperson asked the customer what she *is looking for*. ✗
The salesperson asked the customer what she *was looking for*. ✓

81. Jaya told us that she *will tell* us a story. ✗
Jaya told us that she *would tell* us a story. ✓

82. There is no one in the building *expect* Farid. ✗
There is no one in the building *except* Farid. ✓

83. The *continuous* arguments I have with Vincent are very tiring. ✗
The *continual* arguments I have with Vincent are very tiring. ✓

84. This book is *more easy* to understand than that one. ✗
This book is *easier* to understand than that one. ✓

85. The principal congratulated Mohammad *for* his brilliant performance. ✗
The principal congratulated Mohammad *on* his brilliant performance. ✓

86. He chose *waiting* at the airport. ✗
He chose *to wait* at the airport. ✓

87. This is your favourite flower, *isn't this*? ✗
This is your favourite flower, *isn't it*? ✓

88. The girl *had bowed* as the curtain came down. ✗
The girl *bowed* as the curtain came down. ✓

89. The boy, *aged ten years old*, lived with his grandparents. ✗
The boy, *aged ten years*, lived with his grandparents. ✓

90. The causes of heart disease *is* now well understood. ✗
    The causes of heart disease *are* now well understood. ✓
91. They *all are* nice people. ✗
    They *are all* nice people. ✓
92. How many of us *are owning* more than one car? ✗
    How many of us *own* more than one car? ✓
93. Shashi *has been talking* to Paul a moment ago. ✗
    Shashi *was talking* to Paul a moment ago. ✓
94. If we had wings, we *will have flown* round the world. ✗
    If we had wings, we *would fly* round the world. ✓
95. We plan *eating out* tonight. ✗
    We plan *to eat out* tonight. ✓
96. None of the persons *knows* Shilpa. ✗
    None of the persons *know* Shilpa. ✓
97. The new technology is superior *than* the old one. ✗
    The new technology is superior *to* the old one. ✓
98. Ekta seldom leaves her hometown, *doesn't she*? ✗
    Ekta seldom leaves her hometown, *does she*? ✓
99. Samuel *would apply* for the job if he had seen the advertisement. ✗
    Samuel *would have applied* for the job if he had seen the advertisement. ✓
100. I don't mind *to share* my room. ✗
     I don't mind *sharing* my room. ✓

Appendix 2

Soft Skills

The term 'soft skills' refers to a group of skills and personal qualities that present-day employers look for and value in their employees. Soft skills relate to excellent communication skills, both spoken and written, positive personality traits, social skills and personal attitudes. In this sense, soft skills complement hard skills, which have to do the technical requirements of a job. Hence, you may have the right professional qualifications, be academically brilliant and perhaps even have the required work experience, but you will be successful in an organisation only if you know, for example, how to work as part of a team or how to get along with both your senior and junior colleagues. In other words, soft skills are all about how you deal with people. They are very important in the present-day professional context that requires constant interaction and communication. Thus, it is not surprising that very often, an interviewer talking to two different candidates with equally impressive CVs, decides in favour of the one who seems relaxed, open, friendly and well-adjusted. Of course, a neat and pleasing personal appearance also does make a positive impression in such situations.

While soft skills are acquired early in life and depend to a great extent on the environment in which you were brought up, they can also be consciously learnt. The process could begin either by asking someone who knows you closely to decide whether you possess the soft skills concerned or through doing an honest self-appraisal. You can begin by looking at some of the soft skills recommended by behavioural training experts. See if you have most of the skills listed below, and if you do not, you could try to develop them in the course of your work and interaction with others.

Communication skills

One of the most important soft skills that employers look for is proficiency in the use of language. This means the ability to read, write and speak English (not necessarily the British standard) that can make communication possible. It is, however, not enough to know the mechanics of English—the correct pronunciation, the right words and the appropriate structures. We must also have the skills of knowing when to use standard forms or colloquial expressions, what tone to use in different situations, etc. Oral communication skills include presentation, public speaking and telephone skills while the written forms that you will need to master are writing of reports, official letters and summaries.

Computer skills

The importance of being able to use the basic word processing and presentation software as well as the Internet to get information within a short time and to send emails is very well understood in the present world.

Listening skills

In order to be a good communicator, it is very important that besides being a skilled speaker, you are also a keen, interested listener. Most people fail not because they are unable to state their point of view but because they do not listen to what others have to say.

The right work ethic

This involves the attitude or belief that any work that you undertake to do must be done with sincerity, diligence and a sense of commitment.

Self confidence

You must believe in yourself, and understand your talents as well as your limitations so that you can judge for yourself what tasks you can accept and what you need to say no to. Self-confidence also consists in not shying away from asking questions when you are not clear about something, the willingness to learn from one's mistakes and the ability to take criticism and orders in the right spirit, without feeling humiliated or hurt.

Courtesy and good interpersonal skills

Being polite to everybody at work—senior as well as junior colleagues, clients or visitors—is closely linked to your success at work. Courtesy consists of not only the habitual use of polite expressions such as 'please', 'thank you' and 'excuse me' in speaking to others but also the use of appropriate body language to reinforce your verbal communication. (For example, the words 'Thank you' said in a cold or mechanical manner will not have the effect the words could have if spoken with a smile and in a warm tone.) Courtesy also means respecting other people and their opinions and giving them their due worth.

Capability for team work

This refers to the ability to see yourself as a member of a group with shared aims and responsibilities. It involves sharing your views and ideas with others in your team, discussing work and problems to arrive at the best possible solutions, helping others do their work and also asking for help if you need it. Most importantly, to be an effective member of a team, you must learn to share praise as well as blame with others working with you.

Negotiation skills

While interacting with colleagues as well as with clients and outsiders in an organisation, it becomes necessary to make people agree with your suggestions. Doing this calls for the soft skills of discussing different alternatives as well as persuading and influencing others. This can best be done by learning to use the language used to perform the functions of expressing disagreement politely, persuading and steering people towards decisions that you want them to take (for example, 'Don't you think it would be better if we . . .'). The use of the appropriate body language and tone is also a part of the skill of negotiating.

Self-discipline

It is important to remember that the most effective form of discipline is that which comes from within oneself. Thus, it will help immensely and make work a pleasure if we set and keep to our own strict standards in matters of punctuality, quality of work and loyalty to our employers.

Conformity

The ability to conform to unwritten norms of dress, speech and behaviour at your workplace is one of the skills that will help you succeed there. Remember that you can find ways of conforming to such codes without losing your individuality.

A positive attitude

It is essential to develop a cheerful, optimistic, open and understanding attitude towards people and situations.

Honesty and dependability

These are personal traits that will help you build trust and make friends at work.

Assertiveness

This means standing up for your rights and saying firmly what you believe in without being either passive or aggressive.

Leadership qualities

These involve the ability to take decisions, to take initiative, to motivate and lead by example, to use reason rather than emotion to resolve conflicts, to take blame when things go wrong, to handle emergencies and unforeseen situations, and good organisation skills.

The desire for constant learning and self-improvement

What this means is that, however experienced you are and however much you know, you remain alert and always ready to learn something that you did not know earlier.

Being self-motivated

This is a skill that makes you do things without anybody else reminding you or forcing you to do them.

Managing time

Learning to use your time wisely will help you work faster and better. It involves prioritising tasks to be completed in a day, delegating work and organising work practices better. Managing your time well will help you stay on schedule and meet deadlines.

Handling stress

Unnecessary stress and anxiety will only have a negative effect on your work, and so it is important that you learn how to manage it. You can do this by consciously trying to analyse the reasons for your feeling stressed and also through careful time management and by making sure that you have a healthy diet, exercise and enough time to unwind and relax.

Responding to feedback from others and critiquing others positively

The ability to respond positively to feedback on your work, without either getting defensive without reason or accepting unfair criticism meekly. Similarly, when reviewing the work of others, it is important to be fair and objective, giving praise where it is due and expressing shortcomings clearly but without being offensive or hurtful.

Adaptability

It is not always possible to have similar conditions to work in. You will need to adjust to new situations and learn how to deal with them, often using new methods you have thought of.

Creativity

A highly valued skill, creativity helps you come up with innovative ideas and novel solutions.

The ability to multitask

This soft skill will help you handle several tasks together at one time and also to coordinate between different people.

Appendix 3

Key to the Grammar and Pronunciation Exercises

GRAMMAR

Articles

Exercise 1, p. 6

(a) the (b) a (c) a, an (d) the (e) a, the (f) X (g) X (h) the (i) an, the (j) the, X (k) X (l) the

Exercise 2, p. 7

a. Oranges and lemons are citrus fruits.
b. Asif is going to visit Oxford University.
c. Elephants and lions are found in India.
d. Have you been to the Nilgiri hills?
e. no error
f. You can take the Kerala Express to Shoranur.
g. The children have been sent to bed.
h. The gold you buy here is of excellent quality.
i. Manoj heard an old tale about a unicorn.
j. The philosophy discussed in this book is very difficult to understand.

PREPOSITIONS

Exercise 1, p. 9

(a) on, in (b) for (c) in (d) on, of (e) with, at, in (f) until/till (g) after (h) with, to (i) except for (j) with

Exercise 2, p. 10

a. Between the two sisters, Habiba is the better dancer.
b. They left at midnight for their village.
c. Manu has been living in Dubai for ten years.
d. The shop is below my flat.
e. The girls sat down beside the lake.
f. There is a reference to the drug on page 33 in chapter 6.
g. We insisted on going out for a walk.
h. Don't interfere in my affairs.
i. He was in great need of affection.
j. I am surprised at the slow pace of life here.

Verbs

Exercise 1, p. 12

a. write (action verb)
b. contain (non-action)
c. hope (non-action)
d. want (non-action)
e. believes (non-action)
f. turned (action)
g. washed (action)
h. is (non-action)
i. boarded (action)
j. felt (non-action)

Exercise 2, p. 14

a. picked up (finite), scattered (non-finite)
b. sat (finite), reading (non-finite)
c. stepped (finite), broken (non-finite), cried (finite)
d. entered (finite), soaking (non-finite)
e. trekking (non-finite), is (finite), exciting (non-finite)
f. added (finite), boiling (non-finite)
g. was (finite), to go (non-finite)
h. recommend (finite), brushing (non-finite)
i. longed (finite), to eat (non-finite)
j. gave (finite), wrapped (non-finite)

Exercise 3, p. 15

a. irregular
b. regular
c. regular
d. regular
e. regular
f. regular
g. irregular
h. irregular
i. irregular
j. irregular

Exercise 4, p. 17

a. intransitive
b. intransitive
c. intransitive
d. transitive
e. transitive
f. intransitive
g. intransitive
h. intransitive
i. transitive
j. transitive

Exercise 5, p. 19

a. The verb does not have an object.
b. ball: direct obj.
c. The verb does not have an object.
d. lights: direct obj.
e. door: direct obj.
f. The verb does not have an object.
g. chocolate: direct obj., him: indirect obj.
h. geography: direct obj.
i. Mahabharata: direct obj.
j. The verb does not have an object.
k. The verb does not have an object.
l. father: indirect obj., kurta: direct obj.

Tenses

Exercise 1, p. 21

a. lay, gives
b. work, get
c. store
d. attract
e. produce, take in, give out
f. expand, breathe in, contract, breathe out, have, goes, pumps

Exercise 2, p. 22

lives, works, has, go, teaches, is, paints

Exercise 6, p. 24

a. Indians win the Ranatunga Trophy
b. CM inaugurates computer training centre
(There could be other acceptable responses.)

Exercise 7, p. 25

a. am reading, are making b. is ringing, am taking

Exercise 8, p. 27

a. is visiting, is spending, is travelling
b. is drinking, is eating, is going
c. is arriving, are cleaning up, are painting
d. am spending, am drinking, am eating
e. are marching, is taking, are standing up, is playing

Exercise 9, p. 28

is speaking, is reading out, thinks, has, feel

Exercise 10, p. 30

a. have brushed, have combed, have packed, have eaten, has come
b. have washed, have wiped, have put up, have sent out, have arranged for

Exercise 11, p. 32

a. writes, has been writing, has written
b. have been learning, have learnt, am learning
c. live, have moved, have been, have built, teach, works, is doing, has given, writes, talks, misses

Exercise 12, p. 33

a. (i) was, lived
 (ii) had, sold
 (iii) broke, was, dropped
b. (i) visited, was, fell, returned, has become
 (ii) has painted, painted

Exercise 13, p. 35

lived, used to work, would go/used to go, used to take/would take

Exercise 14, p. 37

a. was taking, saw, was crawling

b. rang, was having, opened, found, was reading
c. walked, saw, were playing

Exercise 15, p. 39

a. had set, left
b. had seen, went
c. posted, had written
d. got, had risen
e. consulted, had worsened

Exercise 16, p. 40

a. builds, has been building, has built, plans, have been asking, sings, has done, became, had dreamt, hopes
b. am, have been teaching, teach, am teaching, is, is expecting, has been, asked, went, is, was, is working, have worked, was, have got/ have been getting, have not accepted

Exercise 17, p. 44

a. is going to be
b. am going to join
c. are meeting
d. is buying
e. is going to return
f. will see
g. are going to fall sick
h. arrives, goes, visits, unveils, returns
i. are visiting
j. will learn

Exercise 18, p. 46

a. will be writing
b. will be traveling
c. will be waiting
d. will be shaking

Exercise 19, p. 47

a. will have saved
b. will have played
c. will have written
d. will have taken
e. will have arrived

Exercise 20, p. 48

a. will have been sleeping
b. will have been attending classes
c. will have been cleaning
d. will have been teaching
e. will have been dancing

Exercise 21, p. 48

a. has keyed in
b. work
c. have been living
d. will have bought
e. rolled
f. was playing
g. will meet you
h. are leaving
i. had broken
j. had been practising

Subject—verb agreement

Exercise 1, p. 52

a. speaks
b. work
c. were
d. were playing
e. has cleared
f. are approaching
g. were staying
h. went
i. paint
j. wants, prefer
k. were, were running, were
l. is moving, has invited, have accepted

Exercise 2, p. 55

a. have
b. were
c. is
d. is
e. knows
f. have collected
g. is
h. needs
i. is admiring
j. happens
k. were looking
l. is falling
m. is
n. have used
o. has

The passive voice

Exercise 1, p. 60

a. The man was acquitted of the crime by the judge.
b. A bouquet of roses and lilies is being made by Nina.
c. All that appear in newspapers is believed (by people).
d. A nest was built by the crows on the jackfruit tree.
e. Dinner will be cooked tonight by my sister.
f. The students had been prepared well by the teacher for the test they took.
g. A bell was being rung by the man outside the store.
h. All the windows have been left open by Maya.
i. Baskets of flowers and sweets were being carried by them.
j. The book will have been read by you by the time I return.

Exercise 2, p. 62

a. Let the lost documents be found.
b. When was the story read by you?
c. Can the tuition fees be paid (by you) tomorrow?
d. Let a bridge be built across the river.
e. Is science fiction read by Lata?
f. Let the injured be carried to the ambulance.
g. Will the fields be flooded by the rising water?
h. When is the gate opened (by them)?
i. Let the bride be sent presents.
j. Is the wound being dressed by the nurse?

Exercise 3, p. 62

a. We will be asked many questions by the doctor.
b. We (or they/everyone) noticed that the attendance in the school was picking up.
c. This toaster can be repaired easily.
d. The Ayurveda College is publishing a book on naturopathy.
e. A man was seen running up to the stage by the people in the auditorium.
f. They have not fed the dogs today. (or Nobody has fed the dogs today.)
g. Timothy's illustrations are praised by everybody.

h. They (or somebody) stole the antique.
i. Can a meeting be set up for us with the director by Bipin?
j. They still deny women the right to vote in some parts of the world.

Direct and indirect speech

Exercise 1, p. 69

a. Hasan said that he was returning to Nagpur the following Saturday.
b. Dr Singh promised that he would bring Jai there if he saw him.
c. Kavita says that the birds are flying away.
d. Her friend said that Helen writes very well.
e. I told the men that they could keep their boxes in the room.
f. Chinnu said that Kurien had built a house in her village the previous year.
g. Everybody will tell them that they did a great job.
h. The officer said that some of the animals had been saved.
i. The teacher said (or explained) that Hitler became the chancellor of Germany in 1933.
j. The woman said that Sania had been looking after her child since the previous day.
k. The director suggested that they have a farewell dinner for their chairperson.
l. Sunita told me that my letter would not reach her as she was leaving the city that day.

Exercise 2, p. 70

a. The nurse asked the patient whether the pain had become worse.
b. Kala asked me if I knew that she was my cousin's colleague.
c. He asked you what the price of that tray was.
d. The boy asked his friends whether they were walking with him to the beach.
e. They asked him where Alka was when the telephone rang.
f. Anju asked Neil which shirt he had sent to the laundry.
g. Everybody will ask her how it felt to be home.
h. The coach asked the athlete whether she practised regularly.
i. The guest enquired why the room was so stuffy.
j. Prem asked his daughter when she could meet him.

Exercise 3, p. 70

a. Tony requested the teacher to give him another day to complete his work.
b. The principal told (or instructed) the student to take the certificates that he had left there two days before.
c. Lola cautioned us against eating fruits and vegetables without first washing them.
d. The general commanded the soldiers to take up positions to defend their camp against the enemy.
e. The pilot ordered that the old people, the women and the children be allowed to go unharmed.
f. Basant exclaimed to his brother that it was fortunate that he was there.
g. The managing director asked Mr Gupta if he would be going to Sri Lanka the following month and informed him that there was an international conference on herbal medicine in Colombo on the 15th.
h. Shruti exclaimed to her mother that it was a pleasant surprise and said that she had been longing to see her.
i. Uncle suggested to Sharan that they leave the car at the service station and said that Uma would pick it up the next evening.
j. Minu asked them to sit down and enquired whether they wanted to speak to her about something.

Exercise 4, p. 71

a. Tania said to her friend, 'Please lend me your umbrella.'
b. They said to me, 'You can take the boat that is going to the Andaman islands.'
c. Padma said, 'Franson, congratulations on your promotion!'
d. The officer said to the passenger, 'Do you have anything to declare?'
e. Shah said, 'My mother will leave tomorrow.'
f. We said to Rashmi, 'We will certainly meet you here (or there).'
g. 'Do you play cards?' he said to me. (or He said to me, 'Do you play cards?')
h. Nita told Shobha, 'I am sorry about losing your bracelet.'
i. The girl said to her brother, 'We are late for the meeting.'
j. Aman said to the salesperson, 'I am looking for Dan Brown's latest novel.'

Negative sentences

Exercise, p. 73

a. I am not a doctor.
b. She does not want to learn ballet.
c. Do not include this amount in your bill.
d. She did not return to India in a month.
e. Basheer is not happy with the arrangements.
f. They do not have a lot of work to complete.
g. Tara was not absent today.
h. Please do not say this to him.
i. The solution was not clear.
j. You did not do Kirti a favour.
k. The boat was not rocking violently.
l. Do not turn the car.
m. Stephen and his friend were not picking guavas from the tree.
n. We will not buy pearls in Hyderabad.
o. They have not been spending a lot on clothes.

Question tags

Exercise 1, p. 75

a. Kranti repaired the clock, didn't she?
b. It is not dark, is it?
c. They were going to the lake, weren't they?
d. The bus had left by the time we got there, hadn't it?
e. You are trying to find someone, aren't you?
f. Pavan has not kept his word, has he?
g. The bread will become soggy, won't it?
h. His parents would not have left before yesterday, would they?
i. I can see how earnest you are, can't I?
j. Shanta loves icecream, doesn't she?
k. The bus skidded on the wet road, didn't it?
l. Vimala sells wooden toys, doesn't she?
m. None of the workers left early, did they?
n. You haven't left the door open, have you?
o. The clothes in the store are priced very high, aren't they?

Exercise 2, p. 76

a. They won't leave the baby alone at home, will they?
b. Cynthia looked pretty in the green dress, didn't she?
c. Gardening used to be Hari's favourite pastime, didn't it?
d. We will grow tomatoes and carrots, won't we?
e. I haven't met the Menons, have I?
f. Mala couldn't run, could she?
g. Mother plans to work late in the office, doesn't she?
h. The astronauts are ready to enter the spacecraft, aren't they?
i. There were ten chocolates in the paper bag, weren't they?
j. The water is getting cold, isn't it?

Simple, compound and complex sentences

Exercise 1, p. 79

a. Kripa will stay either in a hotel or with friends in the city.
b. The clothes were put out in the morning, but they are not dry.
c. Abu is leaving for Chennai today and his father is leaving for Rourkela tomorrow.
d. The boy can rest at home or he can go to school.
e. Arun helped Sally fill in the application form and posted it for her.
f. The workers did an excellent job and so their employer gave them a huge bonus.
g. My dog has neither been active nor has he eaten all day.
h. We were just given an hour to prepare for the test but (still) we did it well.
i. Puneet is not only clever but he is also kind.
j. The problem is complex, yet it is interesting.

Exercise 2, p. 79

a. Tanu was new to the place, yet she got everybody to support her cause.
b. We finished work for the day and left the office.
c. Mini arrived in the morning with a pup in her arms and I was surprised.
d. It was seven in the evening, still it was not dark.
e. Sam walked down the road and looked at the lovely houses on both sides.

f. The students were bored with the hostel food and so they decided to cook a meal for themselves.
g. The weather is bad, so all the flights have been cancelled.
h. Madhu could either work or enrol for an advanced course in computer application.
i. We were exhausted after the climb and so rested on the hilltop for a while.
j. Seema called her uncle and asked him for an address.

Exercise 3, p. 81

a. simple
b. complex
c. simple
d. compound
e. simple
f. simple
g. complex
h. complex
i. complex
j. simple

Exercise 4, p. 82

a. Varkey took me out to lunch when I went to see him.
b. The woman put down the bag that was heavy.
c. I would like to read the poem which my son wrote for his school magazine.
d. The doctor will be able to make an accurate diagnosis if you get the tests done.
e. The guavas are not sweet though they are large.
f. It is our hope that the boy will grow up to be honest.
g. The lecture was so difficult that Maria could not understand it.
h. You cannot reach the fan unless you stand on a stool.
i. Ben peeped into the room where his brothers were sleeping.
j. It is my opinion that the room needs to be painted.

Exercise 5, p. 82

a. Finding the house locked, Farid waited outside for his friend.
b. We missed the bus, yet got to office on time.
c. The squirrels hid the nuts where they usually did.
d. In spite of the curry being far too salty, Amit did not complain.
e. The nurses decorated the ward with flowers and balloons so that it would look bright and cheerful.
f. You can take either the pink sari or the white one.

g. The family sat under a shady tree and enjoyed their picnic lunch.
h. Lily was able to concentrate because there was complete silence in the room.
i. The man in the white kurta speaks fluent Marathi.
j. You must return home before the sun sets.

Pronunciation

Phonetic transcription

Exercise, p. 93

a /zuː/
b /ded/
c /ʃəʊ/
d /lɒt/
e /səʊk/
f /keɪn/
g /tʃeə/
h /pɔː/
i /flaʊə/
j /peɪnt/
k /fɪʃ/
l /ɑːk/
m /beɪk/
n /kɔːl/
o /dæʃ/
p /evə/
q /gæs/
r /bəʊl/
s /tɔːl/
t /hænd/
u /niː/
v /liːk/
w /mɔɪst/
x /nəʊt/
y /wʌn/
z /θriː/

Stress

Exercise 1, p. 96

a. ˈtackle
b. ˈdriver
c. ˈvillage
d. ˈwelcome
e. perˈmit
f. alˈlot
g. deˈvote
h. igˈnore
i. ˈpretext
j. deˈfect
k. ˈcollar
l. ˈdentist
m. ˈmaster
n. ˈpackage
o. ˈnightmare
p. unˈtrue
q. beˈside
r. reˈcourse
s. imˈply
t. alˈlow

Exercise 2, p. 97

a. proˈfessor
b. ˈcalculate
c. imˈportant
d. ˈeducate
e. proˈmotion
f. deˈliver
g. hoˈrizon
h. ˈdelicate
i. ˈrecognise
j. engiˈneer
k. coˈmmittee
l. amˈbition

Exercise 3, p. 98

a. aˈcademy
b. acaˈdemic
c. acadeˈmician
d. bacˈteria
e. bacteriˈology
f. bacterioˈlogical
g. indiviˈdual
h. individuˈality
i. individuaˈlistic
j. ˈpolitics
k. poˈlitical
l. poliˈtician

Exercise 4, p. 99

nouns/adjectives	**verb**
a. ˈproduce	g. proˈduce
b. ˈprogress	h. proˈgress
c. ˈrecord	i. reˈcord
d. ˈsubject	j. subˈject
e. ˈincrease	k. inˈcrease
f. deˈfeat	l. deˈfeat

Exercise 5, p. 100

a. ˈteabag
b. ˈwaterproof
c. ˈwholesale
d. ˈanything
e. ˈbackbone
f. ˈearthquake
g. hot-ˈtempered
h. afterˈnoon
i. halfˈway
j. middle-ˈaged
k. north-ˈwest
l. ˈgoldsmith

Exercise 6, p. 103

a. I ˈparked the ˈcar by the ˈside of the ˈbuilding.
b. The ˈdog ˈjumped into the ˈstream.
c. She is ˈmaking a ˈdress for ˈNaina.

d. Your ˈclasses ˈstart from ˈThursday.
e. ˈGiri ˈsaid that he was ˈtired.
f. The ˈtrees in the ˈforest ˈcaught ˈfire.
g. ˈValsan is my ˈcousin.
h. ˈGive the ˈwooden ˈbox to the ˈman in the ˈwhite ˈshirt.
i. The ˈglass ˈneeds to be ˈwiped.
j. ˈThis is a ˈgovernment ˈdocument.

INTONATION

Exercise, p. 106

a. Good ˋmorning. (falling tone)
b. Where will you ˋstay? (falling tone)
c. This is a ˋjackfruit. (falling tone)
d. Ashwin has applied for a ˋjob. (falling tone)
e. Were the soldiers ˊsafe? (rising tone)
f. Did Bill find his ˊkeys? (rising tone)
g. What a ˊsurprise! (rising tone)
h. When did you move to ˋPathankot? (falling tone)
i. Harish is a ˋlawyer. (falling tone)
j. The house is ˇnearly complete. (Not to worry for it will be ready shortly.) (falling-rising tone)